The church has always venerated the divine scriptures as it has venerated the Body of the Lord, in that it never ceases, above all in the sacred liturgy, to partake of the bread of life and to offer it to the faithful from the one table of the word of God and the Body of Christ.

Dogmatic Constitution on Divine Revelation (Dei Verbum), 21

On the basis of the intention of the Second Vatican Council, the Order of Readings provided by the Lectionary of the Roman Missal has been composed above all for a pastoral purpose. To achieve this aim, not only the principles underlying this new Order of Readings but also the lists of texts that it provides have been discussed and revised over and over again, with the cooperation of a great many experts in exegetical, liturgical, catechetical, and pastoral studies from all parts of the world.

Introduction to the Lectionary for Mass, 58

D1637168

THE WORD OF THE LORD AT MASS

UNDERSTANDING THE LECTIONARY

REGINA A. BOISCLAIR, PhD

LITURGY TRAINING PUBLICATIONS

Nihil Obstat
Very Reverend Daniel A. Smilanic, JCD
Vicar for Canonical Services
Archdiocese of Chicago
June 17, 2015

Imprimatur
Very Reverend Ronald A. Hicks
Vicar General
Archdiocese of Chicago
June 17, 2015

THE WORD OF THE LORD AT MASS: UNDERSTANDING THE LECTIONARY © 2015 Archdiocese of Chicago: Liturgy Training Publications, 3949 South Racine Avenue, Chicago, IL 60609, 1-800-933-1800; fax 1-800-933-7094; e-mail orders@ltp.org. All rights reserved. See our website at www.LTP.org.

Cover: Ambo from Bitonto Cathedral in Italy, 1229. Photo © Adrian Fletcher, www.paradoxplace.com. Used with Permission. This book was edited by Lorie Simmons. Christian Rocha was the production editor, Anna Manhart was the designer, and Luis Leal was the production artist. Photos on pp. 5, 19, and 89 © John Zich. Photo on p. 28: Fourteenth century Italian Lectionary: Irvin Department of Rare Books and Special Collections, University of South Carolina Libraries. Used with permission. Photo on p. 28: Anna Manhart.

Printed in the United States of America.

Library of Congress Control Number: 2015947993

19 18 17 16 15   1 2 3 4 5

ISBN 978-1-61671-245-7

LBWLM

This work is dedicated to

Rev. Gerard S. Sloyan

Priest, Scholar, Teacher, Mentor, Friend,
Lectionary Enthusiast

CONTENTS

"[Christ] is present in his word, since it is he himself who speaks when the holy Scriptures are read in the Church."

Constitution on the Sacred Liturgy (Sacrosanctum Concilium), 7

CHAPTER 1

The Lectionary: Presence and Plan

The Word of God Present among Us

Steeped in the words, images, and stories of the Bible, the Mass recalls to all in the worshiping assembly God's saving works through history, so that Christ and his Paschal Mystery (his dying and rising to new life) become real and present. The first document issued by the Second Vatican Council in 1963, the *Constitution on the Sacred Liturgy (Sacrosanctum Concilium)*, gave us striking insights about the role of Scripture in the liturgy. One of them is that Scripture makes Christ present, not merely through the images it calls up in our imaginations (evocative as those are), but especially as an outward sign of Christ, a sacrament. This presence of Christ we hear with our ears, for "it is he himself who speaks when the holy Scriptures are read in the Church."[1] Christ is present in other ways too (in the priest, the praying and singing assembly of people, and especially in the

---

1   Second Vatican Council, *Constitution on the Sacred Liturgy (Sacrosanctum Concilium)* [hereafter abbreviated as SC], 7.

consecrated bread and wine). In all its words and actions, through the power of the Holy Spirit, the Mass "draws the faithful into the compelling love of Christ and sets them on fire."[2]

> On any given day, the Scripture, prayers, and music in the Mass are all attuned to the moment at which we celebrate—the time within the liturgical year.

> Holy Church celebrates the saving work of Christ on prescribed days in the course of the year with sacred remembrance. Each week, on the day called the Lord's Day, she commemorates the Resurrection of the Lord, which she also celebrates once a year in the great Paschal Solemnity, together with his blessed Passion. In fact, throughout the course of the year the church unfolds the entire mystery of Christ and observes the birthdays of the Saints.[3]

In this way we are always calling to mind the birth, ministry, Death, and Resurrection of Jesus, his Ascension and sending of the Holy Spirit, and his promise to come again as recorded in the Gospel. The Mass is a memorial event that ritually reenacts, renews, enriches, and interprets the words that witness to Christ in the Bible. It is filled with these words, in phrases and hymns that quote or paraphrase biblical passages. Again, the *Constitution on the Sacred Liturgy* sums it up nicely:

> Sacred Scripture is of the greatest importance in the celebration of the liturgy. For it is from Scripture that the readings are given and explained in the homily and that psalms are sung; the prayers, collects, and liturgical songs are scriptural in their inspiration; it is from the Scriptures that actions and signs derive their meaning.[4]

To participate in the celebration of the Mass is to fulfill Christ's instruction: "Do this in memory of me."[5]

---

2 SC, 10.

3 *Universal Norms on the Liturgical Year and the General Roman Calendar*, 1.

4 SC, 24.

5 *The Roman Missal*, Order of Mass; Luke 22:19.

The Liturgy of the Word and the Lectionary

We are most directly aware of the use of the Bible in the readings proclaimed during the Liturgy of the Word. These readings are determined by a list of preselected passages from the Bible and assigned to specific occasions on the Church calendar—the liturgical year. The list of citations for those readings is called a "lectionary," more technically an *ordo*, or order of readings from the Sacred Scriptures. But Catholics also use the term "lectionary" for books that print the readings for Masses in the order in which they are assigned in the liturgical calendar—readings for Masses on Sundays and solemnities, on weekdays and saints' days, and on all other occasions. Often these are divided into different volumes.

A lectionary is not a Bible, which is meant for reading, study, prayer, and meditation. By contrast, a lectionary can be understood as a collection of selections that, when read aloud, become readings or lessons in the liturgy. Whether it provides only the lists of citations or the complete text of the biblical selections, a lectionary does not contain the whole Bible. For example, only between fifty-six to sixty percent of any one of the Gospel accounts is included in the Roman Catholic *Lectionary for Mass* for Sundays and Solemnities. The entire *Lectionary for Mass*,[6] issued by Rome in 1981 and in the United States beginning in 1998, provides for only about ninety percent of the Gospel accounts, fifty-five percent of Acts, the Epistles, and Revelation, and thirteen and a half percent of the Old Testament.[7]

The earliest Christian community, like Jesus, was born with the Scriptures that were sacred to Israel in its crib.[8] The first-century church soon came to favor the Greek translation of those texts,

---

6   Including weekdays, saints' days, ritual Masses such as Baptism, Confirmation, weddings, funerals, and other occasions.

7   *Felix Just, SJ, The Catholic Lectionary Website*, accessed May 5, 2015, http://catholic-resources.org/Lectionary/Statistics.htm. This is an excellent site, full of detailed charts displaying the contents of various editions of the Lectionary.

8   Jews refer to the Scriptures as Tanak, an acronym of its three parts: T = Torah (Pentateuch); N = Nabim (Prophets); K=Kethuvim (Writings).

known as the Septuagint.[9] Over the following two centuries, the Church recognized that certain Christian writings were also inspired by God. By the fourth century the Church had developed the authoritative two-testament canon we call the Bible. (The term "canon" in this instance is the list of texts we identify as Sacred Scripture.) At various times the Church has selected particular passages from that canon for lectionaries. Thus a lectionary is a canon within the canon—a biblical canon for the liturgy.

Designed for the oral proclamation of the Word of God, a lectionary could be considered a "talking book." Just as the Bible is the Word of God conveyed by human authors, lectionary readings are the Word of God conveyed by the human voice. The proclaimed lectionary readings embody the real presence of Christ and invite us to affirm our faith. The ritual pattern within which the readings are proclaimed, the Liturgy of the Word, underscores the relationship between the sacramentality of the Word that is heard and the Sacrament of the Eucharist that is received as Christ's real presence under the appearances of bread and wine. Benedict XVI in *Verbum Domini*, a postsynodal apostolic exhortation concerning Catholic appreciation of the Bible, made this especially clear:

> The sacramentality of the word can thus be understood by analogy with the real presence of Christ under the appearances of the consecrated bread and wine.[10] By approaching the altar and partaking in the Eucharistic banquet we truly share in the body and blood of Christ. The proclamation of God's word at the celebration entails an

---

9   The Septuagint is a Greek translation from Hebrew of the Jewish sacred writings begun in the third century before Christ for the Greek-speaking Jews living outside of Palestine. The term *septuagint* means "seventy" (and so is often abbreviated with the Roman numerals LXX). It comes from a legend that seventy scholars translated the Hebrew texts in seventy days and their translations agreed word for word. The Septuagint includes the Jewish Bible and seven books not included in the Hebrew collection, or canon: Tobit, Judith, 1–2 Maccabees, Wisdom, Sirach, and Baruch, as well as additional sections of Daniel and Esther. The New Testament authors, when quoting the Jewish Scriptures, most often cited the Septuagint. Catholics call its additional books "deuterocanonical" (meaning "second collection") and consider them to be part of the Scripture canon. Protestants call them the Apocrypha and do not accept them in their canon.

10   See *Catechism of the Catholic Church*, 1373–1374.

acknowledgment that Christ himself is present, that he speaks to us,[11] and that he wishes to be heard.[12]

How the Lectionary Differs from the Bible—Selection, Collection, and Liturgical Context

The readings in our *Lectionary for Mass* have been selected and arranged to highlight specific themes and mysteries of the faith, so their message may be somewhat more focused than their meaning in the Bible. Three distinctive features of the Lectionary influence how the readings are heard and understood. First, because they are brief selections taken from longer texts, readings may lack some of the content that would clarify their broader meaning. For example, on the Third Sunday in Ordinary Time, Year C, in the First Reading from Nehemiah 8, we hear a moving description of the priest Ezra reading from the book of the Law to all the people gathered together; he reads from "daybreak till midday." Since we hear only this passage, we do not know that this event is the culmination of the people's return to Jerusalem after the long, agonizing exile. The homily or a commentary may supply that additional information, and that would be interesting, but hearing this passage alone keeps the focus on the great reverence given to the proclaimed Word; we cannot help but catch the similarity between that ancient scene and the liturgy in which we are engaged at this very moment.

Second, the Lectionary is a collection of readings that repositions the selections from their original place in the Bible and places them with other selections taken from their original contexts, creating a new perspective. This change often shifts the meaning they had when in their place in the Bible. For example, the readings for the First Sunday of Lent, Year A, are from Genesis 2 and 3 (the story of

---

11 SC, 7.

12 Benedict XVI, *The Word of the Lord* (*Verbum Domini*), 56.

Adam and Eve succumbing to temptation); Psalm 51 ("Have mercy on me, God . . . ," the sinner's classic confession of guilt and prayer for mercy); Paul's teaching to the Romans from chapter 5 (contrasting Adam, the disobedient son of God [Luke 3:38] who brought sin into the world, with Christ, the obedient Son of God who acquitted the world through the gift of his Passion, Death, and Resurrection); and Matthew's account of Jesus' resistance to the devil's temptation in the desert. When reading the story of Adam and Eve in Genesis, the first book of the Bible, a reader is attending to several themes—certainly to the nature of God, the Creator, as much as to the first act of disobedience. Matthew's account of the temptation of Jesus in the desert comes directly after his baptism and the voice declaring him to be God's "beloved Son." In Jesus' stalwart response to the devil, quoting the Law in Deuteronomy, Matthew unveils more evidence of Jesus' identity as the true and obedient Son. Hearing the reading outside of its biblical context and in the company of the other readings, we will be led to reflect on it in a different way. The compilers of the Lectionary have contrasted Matthew's story of Jesus' victory over temptation with Adam and Eve's failure because they want to make a particular point, for which the excerpt from Paul's Letter to the Romans is the bridge: from Adam's sin, which condemned all of humanity, Christ saves us, and his encounter with the devil demonstrates the obedience that will eventually enable the obedient sacrifice that cancels Adam's sin of disobedience. Each passage, which functions in one way in its biblical context, is lifted and placed in a new arrangement so that it can tell another story about salvation history.

Finally, the original frame for the reading, the Bible as a whole, has been replaced by the context of the liturgical year or calendar. The liturgical year creates the specific way the Church has chosen to

The liturgical year creates the specific way the Church has chosen to be mindful of the story of Jesus on the days the community gathers to celebrate, and it influences the way readings will be heard.

be mindful of the story of Jesus on the days the community gathers to celebrate, and it influences the way readings will be heard. This is especially so during the liturgical seasons of Advent, Christmas Time, Lent, the Sacred Paschal Triduum, and Easter Time. Ordinary Time offers a different sort of frame.[13] During its two periods (winter and summer–autumn), we generally hear semicontinuous reading of each of the three synoptic Gospel accounts (Matthew, Mark, and Luke).[14] Through them, we follow Jesus' story and various themes arise, such as discipleship, mission, and at the end of the liturgical year, the end times. Within Ordinary Time the flow may be interrupted when the date of a major feast or solemnity falls on and has priority over a Sunday.

Through the Lectionary, many selections from the Bible unfold in the frame of the liturgical year, and that affects our interpretation of the readings assigned to these times. For example, on Pentecost Sunday of Year A, the Second Reading is from Paul's First Letter to the Corinthians, in which Paul addresses sinful practices in the community, including pride in one's gifts. In the selection, he speaks of the Spirit as the one source of a diversity of gifts. Although he does not specifically refer to the coming of the Holy Spirit at Pentecost, his description of the gifts illuminates the concrete results of the action and power of the Holy Spirit in our lives. On the Assumption of the Blessed Virgin Mary, the First Reading is a vision from Revelation of a crowned woman giving birth and a dragon waiting to devour the child—a vision that has been interpreted in various ways throughout the Christian tradition. But on this day when heard in the liturgy, the congregation will be thinking of Mary.

---

13 "Ordinary" Time simply means counted time, or an ordered sequence of time.

14 Continuous reading in the Lectionary includes the entire biblical text, one day's reading picking up where the previous one has left off; semicontinuous reading skips over parts of the biblical text so that one day's reading does not pick up exactly where the previous one left off.

In the synoptic Gospel accounts the life of Jesus unfolds in a similar manner, although each of the three accounts has significant differences. (The original Greek word is a combination of *syn*, meaning "together with," and *optic*, meaning "sight." The three accounts see the life of Jesus together, so to speak.) The content of John's account, however, is substantially different.

Our Lectionary—Gift of the Second Vatican Council

The *Lectionary for Mass* used in Catholic communities today is the result of the Second Vatican Council (1962–1965), which brought such remarkable changes to every aspect of the liturgy.[15] Along with all of the rites and ritual books of the liturgy, the Lectionary that had been part of the *Roman Missal* used in the Roman Rite of the Catholic Church since 1570[16] was to be revised and translated into vernacular languages. The chief reason was to include more Scripture in the liturgy. The first document of the Council, the *Constitution on the Sacred Liturgy*, mandated that "the treasures of the Bible . . . be opened up more lavishly, so that a richer share in God's word may be provided for the faithful."[17] The result was an order of readings published in Latin in 1969 as biblical citations only, with accompanying instructions for the episcopal conferences to develop their own vernacular language translations of the readings. In the United States, the *Lectionary for Mass*, including the English Scripture texts, was published in 1970. The new lectionary became mandatory worldwide on the First Sunday of Advent 1971. This Lectionary had three major innovations: (1) it replaced a one-year cycle of readings with a three-year cycle; (2) it provided for three biblical selections as well as a psalm or canticle for each Sunday and solemnity instead of a Gospel passage preceded by a short segment of a New Testament letter called the Epistle; and (3) it included regular readings from the Old Testament that were rarely found in the 1570 order of readings. Even

---

15 Among these were a new focus on the Paschal Mystery as the central focus of every liturgy, an enhanced role for Scripture in the liturgy, the full, active, and conscious participation of the faithful in the liturgy (from which followed permission for the translation of the language used in the Mass from Latin into vernacular languages), and the involvement of the laity in some ministerial roles. See Reverend Joshua R. Brommer, *Imbued with the Spirit of the Liturgy, Ten Insights from Vatican II's Constitution on the Sacred Liturgy* (Chicago: Liturgy Training Publications, 2013).

16 Celebrations of the Extraordinary Form of the Mass still use the Tridentine Missal of 1570.

17 SC, 51.

after the initial volume of the Lectionary was published, the compilers continued to work on the content of that volume, and in 1981 a second edition of the three-year Lectionary for Sundays and Solemnities (in the form of a list of citations) became available.[18] An English Lectionary following the 1981 list was published in Canada in 1992, but due to difficulties in arriving at an English translation satisfactory both to Rome and the United States Conference of Catholic Bishops, the second edition did not make its way to use in the United States until Advent of 1998. That 1998 publication is the one in use today in the United States.

The three-year Lectionary for Sundays and solemnities was accompanied by a two-year Lectionary for weekdays, as well as schedules of readings for saints' days, sacramental and votive Masses, and various pastoral or civic occasions. A complete weekday Lectionary was also an innovation; the 1570 Lectionary provided readings for Sundays, solemnities, saints' days, the sacraments, and weekdays in Lent, but most Masses during the week simply repeated the Sunday readings. Both the three-year Lectionary for Sundays and solemnities and the two-year weekday Lectionary follow the same liturgical calendar, but they are independent from each other.[19]

While some liturgical changes mandated by the Second Vatican Council stirred controversy, the Lectionary never became a focus of disputes. The "new" Lectionary (the three-year Lectionary we use today) greatly enriched the Mass and enhanced preaching; it also fostered a new interest in the Bible among Catholics. In addition, it had and continues to have significant ecumenical influence among English-speaking Anglicans and Protestants.

---

18 Rev. Felix Just, SJ, lists the differences between the 1970 Lectionary and that of 1998 on his extensive website on the Lectionary at *http://catholic-resources.org/Lectionary /Differences-USA1970-1998.htm.*

19 Weekday readings are not intended to relate to those of the preceding or subsequent Sundays.

"In the Liturgy of the Word, the congregation of Christ's faithful even today receives from God the word of his covenant through the faith that comes by hearing, and must respond to the word in faith, so that they may become more and more truly the people of the New Covenant."

Introduction to the Lectionary for Mass, 45

CHAPTER 2

The Lectionary Shapes Our Experience of the Mass

In more ways than many people realize, the Lectionary helps to shape our experience of the Mass, depending on our role in the liturgy.

The Congregation

Considering the prominence of the liturgical readings since the Second Vatican Council, it is astonishing to realize that before the revision mandated by the Council, Bible readings were not such an essential component for the worshiping assembly. Before the revised liturgy that was introduced after the Second Vatican Council, Catholics had come to think that if they arrived before the priest removed the veil covering the chalice before the offertory, they had fulfilled their obligation to attend Sunday Mass. But the Lectionary readings we hear today were chosen to be central to the celebration.

Since the Council, more and more we are participating in a celebration designed to give as much importance to being nourished by the Word as being fed by the Eucharist.

How exactly are we nourished by the Word? While the readings certainly include educational components, the primary purpose of proclaiming them is not to convey information, but to draw us into the stories and teachings of our faith and the mysteries they reveal. During the proclamation of God's Word, we engage in deep, communal listening to the stories of God's love and to his expectations for his people through history. We listen to the teachings and ministry of Jesus, and to stories about the effects of Christian faith. These stories are intended to enter our minds and hearts and to invite our response. Active participation calls us to this work of listening and internalizing the mystery and message of these texts.

Many Catholics have been accustomed to following along in a paperback missal resource in the pews while the readings are proclaimed. This approach is historically rooted in the practice of Catholics during the 1940s and '50s (before the change from Latin to the vernacular, beginning in 1965) who followed the Mass in personal missals that translated the Latin. When the Lectionary was first introduced in 1971, most church-going Catholics knew very little of the Bible, and the use of a resource that introduced the new Mass and new readings was an understandable way to become comfortable with the changes.

After over forty-three years with this Lectionary, most church-going Catholics have become familiar with the readings, at least the readings in the three-year Sunday cycle. Although some members of the congregation still prefer to read along (particularly those with hearing difficulties), many are entering into the practice of listening, particularly if the readers at their parish are strong. Growing familiarity with the Lectionary readings can allow worshiping Catholics to let the message resonate and nourish their minds and hearts. Familiarity can allow the real presence of Christ to be felt, so that the affirmation of faith is sincere, and encourage people to carry the message into ministries and outreach. Familiarity can link God's Good News with all the ways Catholics sense they serve the Gospel of their Lord. Finally, familiarity can inspire an ever-deepening commitment to live the ideals they hear from the Scriptures. Of course, familiarity also carries the potential hazard of allowing people to believe they already know the meaning of a reading, so that they stop listening attentively. Since most who now preach have better training in Scripture than most of the priests who first had to work with the Lectionary, Catholics are coming to grasp that the Lectionary's readings hold ever-new insights, no matter how many times we hear them proclaimed.

Celebrants

The readings, attuned as they are to the day of the liturgical year being celebrated, provide the particular lens for each liturgy and have a great influence on the celebrant's work, whether or not he will preach the homily. For some Masses, the Lectionary provides options for the readings. It may offer the choice between a longer or shorter version of a reading or offer more than one reading from which to choose. Celebrants make those choices, or authorize someone else to do so, and then communicate that information to others whose responsibilities in the liturgy depend on these decisions.[1]

Celebrants will find in the readings the tone, themes, and words that will echo in the prayers they will offer on behalf of the assembly. In addition, after greeting the people at the beginning of the Mass, celebrants may provide a brief introduction to the Mass and its readings to help focus the assembly.

---

1   The *General Instruction of the Roman Missal*, paragraphs 360 and 361, explains the criteria by which these decisions are made.

Homilists

The priest or deacon giving the homily has an awesome responsibility. Homilists pray with the readings, carefully study them in the light of Catholic Scripture scholarship, and discern their meanings in light of the needs of the community. They ask how the readings speak of God's activity, how they use poetic images, and how they suggest faith-filled responses. Many homilists read all the selections for an upcoming season to determine overlapping insights that can be built upon from week to week.

An essential step in preparing the homily is to return to the Bible and read each reading there in its biblical context to understand the intent of the sacred authors. Will the author's intent be clear to the assembly when the reading is heard in the liturgy alongside the other readings and in the context of that day in the liturgical year? Or will the homily need to supply some information about the biblical context of the passages being read? Homilists must also consider if and how the three readings and Responsorial Psalm interpret one another and how they fit into the liturgical year. Since priests and deacons are often pressed with many responsibilities and don't have the time for deep study, or may not have had the education they need, a number of resources are available that summarize the scholarly research on these passages.

Another feature homilists should consider is how the readings may touch on important issues of contemporary concern: ecological issues,[2] poverty and affluence,[3] and respect for life—all significant in the minds of the faithful and Church leaders alike.

---

2   Lawrence E. Mick, *Liturgy and Ecology in Dialogue* (Collegeville, MN: The Liturgical Press, 1997), 81–89; Lisa Dahill, "New Creation: The Revised Common Lectionary and the Earth's Paschal Life," *Liturgy* 27, no. 2 (2012):3–16; Regina A. Boisclair, "Lectionary Selections and Ecological Concerns: A Contribution to Dialogue," *Journal of Ecological Studies* 50, no. 1 (Winter, 2015):77–84.

3   Regina A. Boisclair, "Gospel Lections on Poverty and Affluence in Most Eastern and Western Churches," in *Poverty and Affluence in Judaism, Christianity and Islam*, Nathan Kollar and Muhamma Saharifs, eds. (North Charleston, SC: Createspace, 2015), forthcoming.

Proclaimers of the Word

Those who proclaim the Word[4] to the worshiping assembly also have a serious responsibility and should follow a process of preparation. They are expected to pray with their assigned reading, study its meaning by using various resources, and practice proclaiming it aloud.[5] On Sundays, solemnities occurring on days other than Sunday, and on some feasts, three readings are proclaimed: from the Old Testament, New Testament, and Gospel. It is considered a good practice to assign one reader for each reading. A deacon or priest always proclaims the Gospel. All readers, whether lay or ordained, must be mindful of both the meaning of the text they proclaim and the expressive manner in which they read. Through their proclamation they are conveying the presence of the Lord in the Word. The assembly's response after the First Reading and Second Reading ("Thanks be to God") and after the Gospel reading ("Praise to you, Lord Jesus Christ") is their affirmation of faith in the Lord's presence. Readers are expected to dress with simplicity, modesty, and dignity to honor the Word they proclaim and to avoid distracting the assembly from the proclamation.

Readers proclaim their selections at the ambo from a ritual edition of the Lectionary (or the Gospel may be proclaimed from a separate *Book of the Gospels*, described later). The readings in a ritual edition of the Lectionary are printed in large print and laid out in "sense lines," making the passage look like poetry on the page, each line conveying a coherent phrase that can help guide the reader's phrasing and pauses in the proclamation.

---

4 *Lectors*, strictly speaking, are "instituted lectors"—laymen who have been "instituted" by their bishop. In the absence of instituted lectors, qualified lay women and men may be trained to serve in the ministry of the Word as *readers*. In North America the function of proclaiming the First and Second Readings is most often performed by readers. Proclaiming the Gospel is the role of the deacon, and in his absence, the priest. Only an ordained minister may proclaim the Gospel.

5 Such resources might include biblical commentaries, study Bibles, or a resource designed especially for readers, such as *Workbook for Lectors, Gospel Readers, and Proclaimers of the Word*® published by Liturgy Training Publications.

Through their proclamation, readers convey the presence of the Lord in the Word.

The Introduction to the *Lectionary for Mass* instructs that readers and instituted lectors should be "truly suited and carefully prepared, so that the faithful may develop a warm and living love for Sacred Scripture from listening to the sacred readings."[6] It goes on to describe the preparation they should be given—both spiritual and technical, with a biblical and liturgical formation. It is the responsibility of the parish to provide this training, with the support of the diocese. Even experienced readers should seek ongoing formation. With training, practice, and the help of various resources, readers strive to proclaim clearly and expressively.[7] Although the Lectionary

---

6   Introduction, 55; compare with *General Instruction of the Roman Missal*, 66.

7   In addition to providing brief commentaries on the readings, *Workbook for Lectors, Gospel Readers, and Proclaimers of the Word*® prints the readings in large print for practice, as well as pronunciation aids and advice on tone, expression, pacing, and emphasis. Especially recommended for new readers are *Guide for Lectors* by Virginia Meagher and Paul Turner and *A Well-Trained Tongue* by Aelred Rosser, OSB, also published by Liturgy Training Publications. Even experienced readers will find these to be valuable sources of exercises for proclaiming some of the more challenging selections. They also offer basic information about the literary genres in the Bible, the liturgical year, and the structure of the Lectionary.

includes the Gospel reading, many parishes now own a *Book of the Gospels* (technically, an Evangeliary) that prints the Gospel reading for each Sunday and solemnity. The *Book of the Gospels* is carried in procession and placed on the altar at the beginning of the liturgy. If a vested deacon is serving in the celebration, he carries the *Book of the Gospels*, slightly elevated, and places it with reverence on the altar. If a deacon is not present, one of the readers does so. During the singing of the Alleluia, the Gospel reader, whether deacon or priest, carries the *Book of the Gospels* in procession from the altar to the ambo. Communities develop their own practice for how, when, and where lay readers enter, come to the ambo to proclaim, and return to the assembly. Readers may also read the Universal Prayer (Prayer of the Faithful) or announcements. Occasionally readers proclaim the Responsorial Psalm, but the Introduction to the Lectionary and the *General Instruction of the Roman Missal* recommend that the Responsorial Psalm be sung by the congregation with the leadership of a cantor or psalmist.[8]

Cantors and Psalmists

Those who lead the congregation in song and give melodic voice to the Responsorial Psalm share a long-standing practice with roots in the early synagogue. Cantors (or in the case of the psalm, psalmists) prepare spiritually and musically to lead the congregation in these ancient chanted prayers, staying mindful of the words as they sing the verses and visibly encouraging the congregation to sing the response.

The Lectionary offers the option of using either the psalm assigned to the day or a seasonal psalm that the congregation would come to know well. That decision belongs to the pastor, but the cantor or leader of the music ministry could give good counsel.

While the Responsorial Psalm is led and chanted from the ambo, the Alleluia verse (or during Lent, the verse before the Gospel),

---

8 "As a rule, the responsorial psalm should be sung" (Introduction to the Lectionary, 20); "It is preferable for the responsorial psalm to be sung" (*General Instruction of the Roman Missal*, 61).

chanted before the reading of the Gospel, is not. After the Second Reading the cantor sings the threefold Alleluia, and the congregation responds, repeating it. Then, as the Gospel reader (either deacon or priest) processes with the *Book of the Gospels* from the altar to the ambo, the cantor sings the Alleluia verse, which is followed by another congregational Alleluia response. By this time the Gospel Reader is in place at the ambo, ready to announce the Gospel of the day. This biblical verse assigned by the Lectionary in relation to the Gospel text serves two purposes: it salutes the Gospel and it announces to the assembly one of the important insights they are about to hear proclaimed.

Music Ministers

The rich diversity of music available today for the celebration of Mass makes it possible to find hymns that echo the words and themes of the Lectionary readings. Many parishes vary the style of music at different Masses, but the song lyrics at all Masses should reinforce the biblical texts for each occasion and season. Members of a music ministry, including cantors, would benefit from resources, such as those used by readers, that enhance their understanding of the readings.

Ministers of Liturgical Environment

When worship spaces are effectively designed and thoughtfully adorned, they realize the principle that people remember what they see much better than what they hear. At a minimum, worship spaces must permit people to see, hear, respond, and move with ease. The people's experience of liturgy is enhanced all the more by accents that visually echo the themes of the readings and the season (especially during Advent, Christmas Time, Lent, the Sacred Paschal Triduum, and Easter Time). The Scriptures and the Catholic tradition offer a rich storehouse of symbols, many from the natural world (water, fire, oil, rock, plants, and so forth). In addition, portable statues and icons suited to a specific celebration can stimulate reflection. Plans for enhancing the liturgical environment should always begin with the Lectionary readings since images and symbols found in these texts can be adapted to visually reinforce worship.

Writers of the Prayer of the Faithful or Universal Prayer

The Lectionary readings provide insights and expressions for formulating the Prayer of the Faithful. Often the readings suggest something that we could ask God to help us accomplish, including a change in ourselves.

Since these prayers come immediately after the readings, homily, and Profession of Faith, it is helpful to hear repeated some of the words and ideas that have been introduced in the readings. The verbs in the readings often identify actions that link the readings to local situations. It is also effective to introduce the Prayer of the Faithful with an opening phrase that recaptures one or more points from the readings to affirm what God has already accomplished or promised.[9]

Altar Servers

Before the renewal of the Mass inaugurated by the Second Vatican Council, altar boys voiced responses to the priest celebrant in the place of the people. Today servers (of both genders) respond or sing with the assembly. Still, they remain a very visible witness, and can help foster reverence for the Word of God by the way they attend and respond to it with alert body posture and facial expressions. Servers often carry candles for the procession of the Book of the Gospels from the altar to the ambo and then remain on either side of the ambo during the Gospel's proclamation. They sometimes carry a thurible and offer it to the priest or deacon for reverencing the Book of the Gospels with incense

---

9   Regina A. Boisclair, "The Lectionary: A Resource for General Intersession," *Liturgy: The Journal of the Liturgical Conference* 11, no. 1 (Summer, 1993): 9–13.

Servers help foster reverence for the Word of God. Here they hold candles during the proclamation of the Gospel.

before the proclamation. While these actions are done in silence, each serves to reaffirm Christ's presence in the proclamation.

Leaders of Children's Liturgy of the Word

Those who lead the children's Liturgy of the Word use a simplified but faithful version of the readings that has been authorized for this service (*Lectionary for Masses with Children*). To do this effectively, and to deliver a brief reflection or dialogue with the children, these leaders spend time with the Lectionary readings and with the Bible, working out the meanings and planning how to speak about them with children. Resources designed for this ministry are essential.[10]

---

10 For example, Pat Fossarelli, Donna Eschenauer, and Paul Turner, *How to Lead Children's Liturgy of the Word* (Chicago: Liturgy Training Publications, 2014), and *Children's Liturgy of the Word, a Weekly Resource*, published annually by Liturgy Training Publications. This resource provides scriptural background, identifies connections to Church teachings and traditions, and lays out a plan for the service. It includes appropriate questions, some reflection, and intersessions suitable to both the readings and the children.

Sacristans

Sacristans' duties vary somewhat by parish, but typically they are responsible for preparing and caring for all the elements and articles needed for the celebration of Mass: ritual books, vestments, vessels, the bread and the wine, candles, incense, oil, and so forth. Since the specific day in the liturgical year determines some key details for any Mass, sacristans begin their preparations by consulting the *ordo*, the local diocesan almanac that tells what is being celebrated on each day: whether a Sunday, a simple weekday, an optional or obligatory memorial, a feast, solemnity, or other observance. The *ordo* specifies the liturgical color, indicates options (sometimes the priest must choose which observance to celebrate), tells where to find the prayers for the Mass in the *Roman Missal* (the book that contains the words spoken by the celebrant during Mass), and provides the Lectionary number for the Mass so that the readings in the Lectionary can be located. Sacristans may be responsible for placing the ribbon markers at the appropriate pages in the *Roman Missal* and setting it near the celebrant's chair. They may ensure that the correct volume of the Lectionary is placed on the ambo and open to the First Reading for that Mass. If the *Book of the Gospels* will be used, the sacristan may be responsible for marking the correct page and making sure that the book is ready to be carried in the procession. In order to make these preparations, sacristans must know their way around the Lectionary.

Catechists

Whether or not a parish uses a Lectionary-based catechetical program for faith formation, all catechists should be familiar with the Lectionary so that they will be able to make connections to the Sunday readings. One teaching strategy appropriate for any faith formation group—adult, youth, or elementary school students—is to begin a discussion with the question: What do you remember, what did you take away from this Sunday's readings and the homily?

"From the time of the Apostolic Fathers, the Church has
consistently read the Sacred Scriptures, especially
the Gospels, as an integral part of the
celebration of the Eucharist."

Introduction to the Book of the Gospels, 4

CHAPTER 3

Lectionaries Ancient and New

How did this practice arise—of selecting certain Scripture passages to be read during the liturgy and listing or arranging them in a ritual book?

Jewish Lectionaries

Because the earliest Christians were Jews, they may well have brought some of the liturgical practices they knew from Judaism into their Christian gatherings—particularly the practice of reading from Scripture. So we naturally want to know how Scripture reading was organized in Jewish liturgy. Were there lectionaries?

We know that particular Scripture passages were suggested for reading during Jewish liturgies because they are mentioned in the Old Testament. In Deuteronomy, for example, Moses recommended reading from Torah, the first five books of the Jewish Bible (Old

Testament), every seventh year at the feast of Booths (Deuteronomy 31:10–12). In Nehemiah 8:18 we learn that Ezra read to the people from the book of the Law "day after day" during the feast of Booths. Josephus, the first-century Jewish historian, implies that the Septuagint, (the translation into Greek of the Jewish Bible plus the seven additional books not included in the Jewish canon), was produced for reading in the synagogues of the Greek-speaking communities outside of Palestine.[1]

We also find evidence for Scripture reading in Jewish liturgies in the New Testament. Luke, writing in the Acts of the Apostles (15:21), claims that reading from the Torah in the synagogues on the Sabbath was a universal feature in the first century, and in Acts 13:15 he indicates that the Sabbath readings also included a selection from the prophets. In his Gospel account, Luke reports that Jesus read Isaiah 61:1–2 in the synagogue of Nazareth on the Sabbath (4:17–20), but we will never know whether the passage from Isaiah was assigned by a lectionary. There is evidence of "a list of continuous readings of the Torah for Sabbaths, festivals and also Mondays and Thursdays," dating from a hundred years before Christ,[2] and it may be that public reading of assigned passages from the Torah and the Prophets was an ancient practice.[3] There is more direct evidence that for particular Jewish feasts, such as Passover, Rosh Hashanah, and Purim, the passages describing the events being commemorated were assigned to those particular feasts.[4]

Apart from particular selections suited to a particular fast or feast, Torah portions (readings from the Torah) were, and still are, continuous—the reading assigned to the following occasion picks up precisely where the last one left off. Torah portions are still coupled

---

1 Josephus writes about this in his defense of Judaism, *Against Apion*, 2:18.

2 John Reuman , "A History of Lectionaries: From the Synagogue at Nazareth to Post-Vatican II," *Interpretation* 31 (April, 1977): 118.

3 That seems to be the assumption of the *Mishnah*, an authoritative collection of oral teaching and exegesis of the Jewish Law, which is dated at around AD 200. Jacob Neusner, trans., *The Mishnah* (New Haven and London: Yale University Press, 1980), 320–1.

4 Ibid.

with a reading from the prophets (called a Haftorah portion) that has been selected to correspond to the passage from the Torah with which it was assigned.

At the time of Jesus and in the early years of the Christian communities there were at least two lectionaries in use within Judaism. However, a three-year Palestinian lectionary with both Torah and Haftorah portions was gradually replaced by the one-year lectionary that originated in the Jewish community in Babylon which also assigned two readings.

This description of Jewish lectionaries shows that some of the very same features in our current Roman Catholic Lectionary were found in Jewish lectionaries before the time of Jesus. Selecting readings to suit an observance, selecting readings to correspond one to another, assigning continuous readings from Scripture, and spreading the assignments over a set period of time, after which they will be repeated—are all features of the lectionaries of Israel that are found in similar ways in our contemporary Roman Catholic Lectionary.

Christian Lectionaries up to 1570

We do not know for certain if the earliest gatherings of the Jesus movement read from the Scriptures of Israel while they continued to worship in the Temple and attend synagogues. Although different early Christian communities had very different practices, there can be no doubt that once Jewish Christians left or were expelled from the synagogue, some came to include the practice of reading from Scripture during their Christian gatherings. It is also fair to conclude that once a community began to include readings from the Scriptures of Israel, they soon added readings from Christian writings. In some places it is possible that the reading of Christian writings was introduced even before the Scriptures of Israel were read. When St. Paul first wrote to the Thessalonians, (in about AD 50), he instructed them to read his letter to the community (1 Thessalonians 5:27). First Thessalonians was the very earliest Christian writing to find its way into the New Testament, and it instructs the gathered Christians to listen to it being read aloud.

Brief remarks in the writings of people from the first few centuries are the only clues to what Scriptures were read in Christian communities. Justin Martyr, the martyred theologian of the second century, indicates that "memoirs of the apostles or the writings of the prophets" were proclaimed, "as long as time allows."[5] (Not surprisingly, this practice was modified.) From Cyprian, the early third-century Bishop of Carthage, also a martyr, we learn that in his time individuals were ordained to the office of reader.[6] A fourth-century document called the *Apostolic Constitutions* identifies a five-reading sequence "of the law and the prophets, of our epistles and the Acts as well as the Gospels."[7]

The selection of which texts would be read at what times continued to vary from community to community, but some standard choices emerged as specific feasts and seasons developed in the liturgical year. From the beginning, Sunday, the day of the Lord's Resurrection, was especially significant to Christians, as numerous New Testament passages tell us.[8] By the second century, Pliny the Younger, a Roman magistrate, writes that Christians in the territory he governs are meeting regularly on Sunday. Other writings of that time testify to an annual commemoration of the Passion, Death, and Resurrection of Christ called the Pasch, which occurred around the same time as the Jewish Passover.

Once Emperor Constantine legalized Christianity so that Christians were no longer be persecuted in the Roman Empire (in 313),

The selection of texts to be read continued to vary from community to community, but some standard choices emerged.

---

5   *First Apology*, 67.

6   *Epistle*, 20:4.

7   8:5:11.

8   Such as Matthew 28:1ff. and 28:9; Mark 16:1ff.; Luke 24:1ff., 24:13, and 36; and John 20:19 and 22.

Christian communities began to build public houses of worship and more official liturgical practices developed. In 325 Constantine called the Council of Nicaea to establish consensus on a basic theological issue: the nature of the Son and his relationship to the Father. Another concern discussed at that Council was a controversy about how to determine the date of Easter. That a common date for Easter was so vital to all Christians tells us that key elements of a liturgical year were becoming established. All other feasts and commemorations would relate to this central feast of the Lord's Resurrection, and from the developing calendar of feasts, a plan for liturgical readings would follow.

Such plans would undergo many modifications. In the fifth century, Rome, the dominant influence for the western Church, and Constantinople, the dominant influence for the eastern Churches, reduced their readings from five to three lessons. In the sixth century, Rome reduced the readings to two, and Constantinople did the same in the seventh century. In the West, once the readings were reduced to two, the First Reading came to be called "the epistle" even when the selection was from the Old Testament, Acts, or the Book of Revelation, since most of these first readings did come from one of the epistles of the New Testament.

Between the fourth and seventh centuries, then, a course of liturgical readings extending through an entire year emerged along with a calendar for the liturgical year. What physical form did these plans take? How did lectors find the readings they were supposed to proclaim? Early manuscripts and books show that readings were indicated in three different ways. One was to place markings in the margins of Bibles showing where to begin and end a reading. The divisions of the books of the Bible that we know, into chapters and verses, were not developed until later centuries, except for the Gospel accounts, which were divided into sections by numbers. The second way of designating readings was through a list giving the day and month on which a reading should be read, the name of the liturgical day, the name of the book of the Bible (with the section number if from a Gospel), and the beginning words of the reading (*incipit*), the word *usque* (meaning "up to"), and the ending words of the reading (*explicit*). The third method was to collect in a book the actual texts to be read in the order of the liturgical days of the year on which they would be read—similar to the form of Lectionary we use today. The oldest Lectionary to come down to us is fifth-century Armenian lectionary that reflects the plan of readings used in Jerusalem in the early fifth century.[9]

While other rites have existed in the western Church (Ambrosian, Galican, Celtic, Mozarabic, and so forth) the Roman Rite has always predominated. Gradually, over the years, lectionaries used in Rome made their way to France or Germany, were modified, returned to Rome, only to be sent back again and to return with new modifications. This Roman-Frankish-Germanic mixture is reflected in the eighth century *Lectionary of Murbach*, which is considered the parent to the Lectionary incorporated in the Tridentine *Roman Missal* of 1570. The Tridentine Lectionary, or one very similar, was used throughout Europe and Britain even after the Reformation, since at the time, traditional Lutheran and Anglican lectionaries were almost identical to that of Rome.

The Tridentine Lectionary

The Council of Trent (1545–1563) left liturgical reform to the pope, and Pope Pius V authorized the Roman Missal, which included what has come to be known as the Tridentine Lectionary. This Lectionary provided a one-year cycle of Gospel readings together with a second reading that was called the Epistle. (See Table 1 for a listing of the Sunday readings.) The Gospel readings were suitable for solemnities (Christmas, Easter, Pentecost, and so forth) or for the themes associated with the liturgical seasons (Advent, Christmas Time, Lent, and Easter Time) as they were understood in the sixteenth century. The Gospel selections for the many Sundays after Pentecost represent a

---

9   See http://www.bombaxo.com/renoux.html, accessed July 28, 2015.

A fourteenth century Lectionary from Italy. Red lettering identifies the reading that follows (*Sed'm matheus*: according to Matthew). The reading begins at the large initial I: "In those times . . . "

haphazard group of accounts from Jesus' ministry drawn from the Gospel that was considered to offer the most complete story of a particular episode. Some of the "Epistles" in this Lectionary appear to have been chosen to suit the occasion; others appear to have been suggested by the Gospel passage. However, most of the first readings in the Tridentine Lectionary seem to be the remnant of an earlier semicontinuous system of readings without any connection to the Gospel with which they are collected or to the occasion to which they were assigned. The rare readings from the Old Testament were assigned to a few feasts, vigils, ember days,[10] and some octave

10 Ember days in the Tridentine Lectionary were days set aside for fasting in preparation for the four important commemorations of the year—Christmas, Lent, Pentecost, and Exaltation of the Holy Cross.

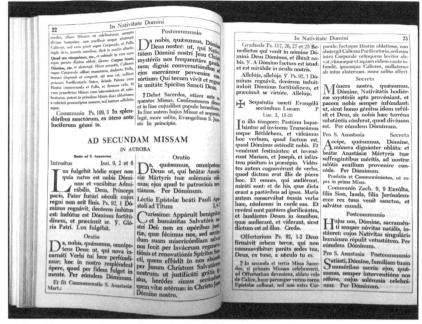

Pages from the Tridentine *Roman Missal*, Mass at Dawn, reading: Luke 2:15–20.

(eight-day) celebrations. Statistically, the 1570 Lectionary included approximately twenty-two percent of the Gospels, eleven percent of the Epistles, and less than one percent of the Old Testament, other than the psalms.[11]

Needed: A New Lectionary

In the late nineteenth and early twentieth centuries, a deep interest in the liturgy was growing both in Benedictine monasteries and in academic circles. This liturgical movement recognized that additions to the liturgy introduced over the centuries had rendered public worship remote from and incomprehensible to most Catholics.

---

11 These statistics come from the excellent website of Rev. Felix Just, SJ, "The Catholic Lectionary Website," (http://catholic-resources.org/Lectionary/Overview.htm). Although the Tridentine Lectionary was replaced by the Lectionary devised in fulfillment of the mandate of the Second Vatican Council, it is still used in celebrations of the Latin Extraordinary Form of the Mass as well as its variant in the special Latin rites of various orders, such as the Dominicans, which are celebrated in various places.

Table 1

One-Year Cycle of Readings for Sundays in the Tridentine Lectionary

Sunday, Solemnity, or Feast	Reading I	Gospel
First Sunday of Advent	Romans 13:11–14a	Luke 21:25–33
Second Sunday of Advent	Romans 15:4–13	Matthew 11:2–10
Third Sunday of Advent	Philippians 4:4–7	John 1:19b–28
Fourth Sunday of Advent	1 Corinthians 4:1–5	Luke 3:1–6
Nativity of the Lord: Vigil	Romans 1:1–6	Matthew 1:18b–21
Nativity of the Lord: Night	Titus 2:11–14	Luke 2:1–14
Nativity of the Lord: Dawn	Titus 3:4–7	Luke 2:15–20
Nativity of the Lord: Day	Hebrews 1:1–12	John 1:1–14
Sunday within the Octave of Christmas	Galatians 4:1–7	Luke 2:33–40
Octave of Christmas	Titus 2:11–15	Luke 2:21
Sunday after the Octave Day of the Nativity	Acts 4:8–12	Luke 2:21
Epiphany of the Lord	Isaiah 60:1–6	Matthew 2:1–12
Holy Family of Jesus, Mary, and Joseph	Colossians 3:12–17	Luke 2:42–52
Second Sunday after Epiphany	Romans 12:6–16	John 2:1–11
Third Sunday after Epiphany	Romans 12:16b–21	Matthew 8:1–13
Fourth Sunday after Epiphany	Romans 13:8–10	Matthew 8:23–27
Fifth Sunday after Epiphany	Colossians 3:12–17	Matthew 13:24–30
Sixth Sunday after Epiphany	1 Thessalonians 1:3–10	Matthew 13:31–35
Septuagesima Sunday	1 Corinthians 9:24—10:5a	Matthew 20:1–16
Sexagesima Sunday	2 Corinthians 11:19–33; 12:1–9	Luke 8:4–15
Quinquagesima Sunday	1 Corinthians 13:1–13	Luke 18:31–43
Ash Wednesday	Joel 2:12–19	Matthew 6:16–21
First Sunday in Lent	2 Corinthians 6:1–11	Matthew 4:1–11
Second Sunday in Lent	1 Thessalonians 4:1–7	Matthew 17:1–9
Third Sunday in Lent	Ephesians 5:1–9	Luke 11:14–28
Fourth Sunday in Lent	Galatians 4:22—5:1a	John 6:1–15
Passion Sunday	Hebrews 9:11–15	John 8:46–59

Sunday, Solemnity, or Feast	Reading I	Gospel
Palm Sunday	Philippians 2:6–11	Matthew 26:1—27:66
Holy Thursday	1 Corinthians 11:20–32	John 13:1–15
Good Friday	Hebrews 9:11–15 Exodus 12:1–19	John 18:1—19:42
Easter Vigil	Genesis 1:1—2:2 Genesis 5:32—8:21 Genesis 22:1–19 Exodus 14:15—15:2 Isaiah 54:17—55:11 Baruch 3:9–38 Ezekiel 37:1–14 Isaiah 4:1–6 Exodus 12:1–11 Jonah 3:1–10 Deuteronomy 31:23—32:4 Daniel 3:1–24 Colossians 3:1–4	Matthew 28:1–7
Easter Sunday	1 Corinthians 5:7–8	Mark 16:1–7
Octave of Easter	1 John 5:4–10	John 20:19–31
Second Sunday after Easter	1 Peter 2:21–25	John 10:11–16
Third Sunday after Easter	1 Peter 2:11–18	John 16:16–22
Fourth Sunday after Easter	James 1:17–21	John 16:5–14
Fifth Sunday after Easter	James 1:22–27	John 16:23–30
Ascension of the Lord	Acts 1:1–11	Mark 16:14–20
Sunday after the Ascension	1 Peter 4:7b–11	John 15:26—16:4a
Pentecost Sunday	Acts 2:1–11	John 14:23–31
Feast of the Most Holy Trinity	Romans 11:33–36	Matthew 28:18–20
Second Sunday after Pentecost	1 John 3:13–18	Luke 14:16–24
Third Sunday after Pentecost	1 Peter 5:6–11	Luke 15:1–10
Fourth Sunday after Pentecost	Romans 8:18–23	Luke 5:1–10
Fifth Sunday after Pentecost	1 Peter 3:8–15a	Matthew 5:20–24
Sixth Sunday after Pentecost	Romans 6:3–11	Mark 8:1–10a
Seventh Sunday after Pentecost	Romans 6:19–23	Matthew 7:15–21
Eighth Sunday after Pentecost	Romans 8:12–17	Luke 16:1–9

Sunday, Solemnity, or Feast	Reading I	Gospel
Ninth Sunday after Pentecost	1 Corinthians 10:6–13	Luke 19:41–47a
Tenth Sunday after Pentecost	1 Corinthians 12:2–11	Luke 18:9–14
Eleventh Sunday after Pentecost	1 Corinthians 15:1–10	Mark 7:31–37
Twelfth Sunday after Pentecost	2 Corinthians 3:4–9	Luke 10:23–37
Thirteenth Sunday after Pentecost	Galatians 3:16–22	Luke 17:11–19
Fourteenth Sunday after Pentecost	Galatians 5:16–24	Matthew 6:24–33
Fifteenth Sunday after Pentecost	Galatians 5:25—6:10	Luke 7:11–16
Sixteenth Sunday after Pentecost	Ephesians 3:13–21	Luke 14:1–11
Seventeenth Sunday after Pentecost	Ephesians 4:1–6	Matthew 22:34b–46
Eighteenth Sunday after Pentecost	1 Corinthians 1:4–8	Matthew 9:1–8
Nineteenth Sunday after Pentecost	Ephesians 4:23–28	Matthew 22:1–14
Twentieth Sunday after Pentecost	Ephesians 5:15–20	John 4:47–53
Twenty-First Sunday after Pentecost	Ephesians 6:10–17	Matthew 18:23–35
Twenty-Second Sunday after Pentecost	Philippians 1:6–11	Matthew 22:15–21
Twenty-Third Sunday after Pentecost	Philippians 3:17—4:3	Matthew 9:18–26
Twenty-Fourth Sunday after Pentecost	Colossians 1:9–14	Matthew 24:15–35

At the same time Catholic biblical scholars were gradually allowed to study Scripture in its historical contexts and to undertake research which resulted in archaeological, historical, and textual discoveries. New understandings of the Bible led many to realize that the existing 1570 Lectionary deprived Catholic Christians of their full biblical heritage.

In contrast to Church officials in charge of liturgy at that time, who considered the Mass the concern of priests and not the people, liturgical theologians and Catholic Scripture scholars alike wanted rites that encouraged the participation of the people. Both groups greatly influenced the Second Vatican Council.

The Council's very first document, *The Constitution on the Sacred Liturgy* (*Sacrasanctum Concilium*) issued in 1963, called for "more reading from holy Scripture and it is to be more varied and apposite" (35.1). The document also asked that "a more representative portion of holy scripture will be read to the people in the course of a prescribed number of years" (51).

The overall arrangement of the liturgical year had been fairly standard since the seventh century.[12] In the west it began four Sundays before Christmas with Advent, followed by the short Christmas season which ended at Epiphany. Then depending on the date of Easter, there would be some Sundays after Epiphany, followed by a three-week span just before Lent that ended with Holy Week. That was followed by the Sundays of Easter that concluded with Ascension Thursday and Pentecost that landed somewhere in the late spring, followed by however many more Sundays were left until Advent. However, by the 1960s, the Catholic calendar was cluttered with many saints' days and their octaves. When saints' days fell on a Sunday, many were given priority over the regular Sunday cycle so that much of the basic story of Jesus was lost. *The Constitution on the Sacred Liturgy* asked that the new calendar of Sundays and solemnities concentrate on "the whole mystery of Christ from his incarnation and birth until his ascension, the day of Pentecost, and the expectation of blessed hope and of the Lord's return."[13]

The Consilium

In January 1964, Pope Paul VI established the Council for the Implementation of the Sacred Liturgy. The work of this body, which

---

12 Advent (four Sundays before December 25), Christmas–Epiphany, after Epiphany, Lent, Holy Week, Easter–Pentecost, after Pentecost.

13 SC, 102.

came to be known as the Consilium, was divided into fourteen study groups. Group I was charged with revising the calendar of the liturgical year; group XI was charged with revising the Lectionary for the new calendar.

The revised liturgical year was an essential prelude to work on the Lectionary. (For a visual sense of the changes, compare table 1 with table 2.) Following the mandate in the *Constitution on the Sacred Liturgy*, the new liturgical year allows "the whole mystery of Christ"[14] (his Paschal Mystery) to stand out more boldly than it could in the earlier calendar, when so many observances of saints had proliferated. To accomplish this, the new calendar gives precedence to the "Proper of Time" over the "Proper of Saints." The Proper of Time includes all the days and seasons of celebration focused on Christ. Paramount are the weekly celebrations of Sunday, the "little Easter" day of Christ's Resurrection, and the annual celebration of seasons and days. The center of the year is the Holy Paschal Triduum commemorating the Lord's Passion, Death, and Resurrection, with its preceding period of preparation, Lent, and Easter Time, the fifty days of celebration and unfolding of the mysteries after Easter Sunday. Next in importance is Christ's Incarnation, celebrated on the day of the Nativity of the Lord along with its related days at Christmas Time and the period of preparation preceding it, Advent. The Sundays between the seasons, during Ordinary Time, continue to focus on Christ's life, teaching, and saving sacrifice. Intertwined with the Proper of Time is the Proper of Saints—a reduced but still plentiful number of days celebrating the saints.

The center of the year is the Holy Paschal Triduum commemorating the Lord's Passion, Death, and Resurrection.

In contrast to the calendar before the Council, the highest-ranking solemnities and feasts (most related to the Lord and some to the

---

14 SC, 102. (All of chapter 5 pertains to the liturgical year.)

saints) were fewer and only some of these were given priority over the Sunday cycle. Bishops' conferences could decide which would be obligatory for their areas.[15] The new calendar removed all octave observances, except for Easter and the Nativity of the Lord,[16] as well as the three-week pre-Lenten season of "Gesima Sundays."[17] It also restored an ancient tradition of following Epiphany with a commemoration of the Baptism of the Lord; it transferred the Solemnity of Our Lord Jesus Christ, King of the Universe, from the last Sunday in October to the Last Sunday of the Year, which allowed that solemnity to assume the eschatological thrust that traditionally marked the end of the liturgical year.[18] The revised liturgical year provided the frame of the new Lectionary.

---

15 In the United States, Holydays of Obligation include the following solemnities: in addition to all Sundays, the Solemnities of the Nativity of the Lord (December 25), Mary, the Holy Mother of God (January 1), the Ascension of the Lord (which in some areas of the United States is transferred to the following Sunday but in others is still celebrated on Thursday), the Assumption of the Blessed Virgin Mary (August 15), All Saints (November 1), and the Immaculate Conception of the Blessed Virgin Mary (December 8). They are obligatory no matter when they fall during the week, and they also have precedence over the regular Sunday observance if their dates fall on Sunday. The following have precedence over Sunday if the dates on which they fall are on a Sunday: St. Joseph (March 19), the Annunciation of the Lord (March 25), the Nativity of John the Baptist (June 24), Sts. Peter and Paul (June 29), the Transfiguration of the Lord (August 6), the Commemoration of All the Faithful Departed (All Souls, November 2), and the Dedication of St. John Lateran (November 9). When these dates do not fall on a Sunday they are not obligatory Holydays.

In Canada, aside from Sundays, Holydays of obligation are the Nativity of the Lord (December 25) and Mary, the Holy Mother of God (January 1).

16 Octave observances are those celebrated for a full eight days; they continue the celebration of a solemnity, feast, or memorial for the eight days after its calendric observance. These had proliferated until they were reduced to three (Christmas, Easter, and Pentecost) by Pope Pius the XII in 1955. The 1969 revision eliminated the old Octave of Pentecost, leaving only two.

17 The three Sundays before Lent had been called Septuagesima, Sexagesima, and Quinquagesima.

18 National and regional bishops' conferences have been given permission to transfer some important observances that fall on a specific date to a Sunday. Thus, in the United States, Epiphany (January 6) is observed in place of the Second Sunday after Christmas, Ascension Thursday (forty days after Easter) is observed in some regions of the United States in place of the Seventh Sunday of Easter, and the Most Holy Body and Blood of Christ (Corpus Christi, Thursday following Trinity Sunday) is observed on the Sunday that follows the Feast of the Most Holy Trinity.

"The liturgical books are to be revised as soon as possible. Experts are to be employed on this task, and bishops from various parts of the world are to be consulted."

Constitution on the Sacred Liturgy (Sacrosanctum Concilium), 25

CHAPTER 4

Designing the Lectionary

Foundational Ideals

While the Second Vatican Council neither considered how a new Lectionary should be devised nor specified what it should contain, it did express ideals for its content and formulation. By stipulating that the biblical readings must be (1) incorporated as an essential part of liturgy (SC, 7, 24, 33, 35); (2) prioritized by observances of the Lord's Day, solemnities, and seasons (SC, 49, 102, 106, 107); and (3) include a significant amount of the Bible (SC, 35.1, 51), the Council expressed its general desire concerning the function, form, and contents of the Lectionary. By indicating that the new Lectionary must (4) take into account contemporary pastoral concerns (SC, 4, 23, 37–40, 107), and (5) honor liturgical traditions of the past (SC, 107), the Council identified what should be taken into consideration while formulating a new Lectionary.

Study group XI (responsible for the Lectionary) determined that the foundational principle for devising the new Sunday Lectionary would be as follows:

"The mystery of Christ and the history of salvation" [SC, 16] must be presented in the readings . . . [such that] the new system of readings must contain the whole nucleus of the apostolic preaching about Jesus as "Lord and Christ" (Acts 2:36) who fulfilled the Scriptures by his life, his preaching, and, above all, his paschal mystery and who gives life to the Church until his glorious return.[1]

It took three years to prepare resources, consult biblical scholars, hold discussions, and devise preliminary schemas. Rev. Gaston Fontaine, the Canadian secretary to study group XI, prepared tables of fifty Catholic and non-Catholic lectionaries, ancient and modern, from both eastern and western churches, to identify which readings were used in the past and when. Biblical scholars were asked to identify passages from the Bible that they sensed were suited to liturgical proclamation, to identify those they believed merited a Sunday assignment, and to suggest the season or observance to which some were especially appropriate. Their lists, drawn from every book in the Bible, were then sent to catechetical and pastoral theologians for comment. A preliminary draft of the Sunday Lectionary was produced in 1967. Bishops worldwide and over eight hundred international experts in Scripture, liturgy, catechesis, and pastoral care examined this draft. After that consultation, a final revision eliminated some difficult passages, added other passages, and improved the divisions of the selections. Additional readings were assigned for the Sundays in Lent, some major feasts were changed, and alternative Gospels were assigned to some solemnities.[2]

Decisions

To accomplish the task, decisions had to be made: the number of years, the number of readings, the order in which books would be introduced, how collections were to be established, what to omit, and

---

1   Annibale Bugnini, *The Reform of the Liturgy 1948–1975*, trans. Matthew J. O'Connell (Collegeville, MN: Liturgical Press, 1990), 410.

2   Bugnini, 420.

what to emphasize. These decisions determined the structure and content of the new Sunday Lectionary.

At first some felt that the old Lectionary might be retained as one year of a multiyear system, since both Anglican and Lutheran lectionaries were very similar. However, when asked their opinion, the Protestant and Anglican observers to the Consilium advised against holding on to the old Lectionary. Their churches also intended to revise their lectionaries and were awaiting the results of the Catholic effort.[3] It was soon recognized that a multiyear Lectionary should follow the same pattern every year.

A Three-Year Sunday Lectionary

Although some wanted a four-year Lectionary for Sundays and solemnities, they chose to develop a three-year cycle, to associate each year with a synoptic Gospel account, and to supplement every year with selections from the Gospel according to John. Matthew was designated as the Gospel for Year A, Mark for Year B, and Luke for Year C. John would be assigned to several Sundays during Lent and Easter Time, a number of festival days every year, and as a supplement to the short Gospel account of Mark in Year B. The new plan allowed for variety, since it included many passages from different books of the Bible, but also continuity, in that all years followed the same themes during the seasons of the liturgical year, the same recurring solemnities and feasts, and the same privileging of Sundays.[4]

Already in 1955, under the leadership of Pope Pius XII, the Sacred Paschal Triduum had been restored and significant changes had been introduced to the observances of Holy Week. Everyone, including those charged with revising the liturgy, recognized that those efforts were satisfactory, so the readings assigned to those

---

3   Bugnini, 200–2. This was the only occasion on which Anglican and Protestant observers as a group were formally asked for their opinion.

4   Normand Bonneau, *The Sunday Lectionary: Ritual Word, Pascal Shape* (Collegeville, MN: Liturgical Press, 1998), 37–38.

days were retained in the new Lectionary, with only one exception: the Gospel account of Christ's Resurrection at the Easter Vigil was changed to follow the synoptic Gospel assigned to each year (Matthew, Mark, or Luke).

(See table 2 at the end of the next section about the Gospel Readings for a complete listing of the Sunday readings in the new three-year cycle.)

The Gospel Readings

Just as the Sunday Lectionary was considered the most important part of the Lectionary revision, the assignment of Gospel passages was considered the most important decision to be made about readings. Apart from Ascension and Pentecost, when the stories told come from the Acts of the Apostles, all the other solemnities that commemorate central aspects of Jesus' life are recorded in the Gospel accounts. Gospel readings were selected for Christmas Day and the Sundays in Easter Time, as well as for the Annunciation of the Lord (March 25), the Transfiguration of the Lord (August 6), and other solemnities. Some, such as most Sundays and solemnities during Christmas Time, are identical every year.[5] Others, like those in Easter Time, take good advantage of the three-year cycle. The Gospel for the Easter Vigil comes from the accounts of the women's discovery of the empty tomb in the synoptic Gospel of the year, be it A, B, or C, and John's account of the empty tomb is assigned to Easter Sunday every year, although the Lectionary also allows for the use of the Easter Vigil Gospel on Easter Sunday.

The seasons of Advent, Lent, and Easter Time had long been associated with a number of conflicting themes. In devising the new Lectionary, choices were made among these themes to provide consistency and a sharper focus so that the Gospel readings would

---

5   Christmas has four Masses: Vigil, Night, Dawn, and Day. The Gospel for the Vigil is from Matthew, those for Night and Dawn are from Luke, and the Gospel for the Day is the prologue of John.

underscore the most appropriate concept(s) for each season. For example, in the 1570 arrangement, Advent began with anticipation of the Second Coming of the Lord on the First Sunday and made note of the upcoming commemoration of Jesus' birth on the ember days that fell in Advent's third week.[6] On the Second, Third, and Fourth Sundays of Advent the emphasis was on penitence. In the renewal of Advent, the penitential note is eliminated. Gospel readings are chosen to highlight a joyful anticipation of Christ's Second Coming during the first week and the ministry of Christ's herald, John the Baptist, in the second and third week, leading to the anticipation of the upcoming commemoration of Jesus' birth.

The seasons of Advent, Lent, and Easter Time had long been associated with a number of conflicting themes. In devising the new Lectionary, choices were made among these themes to provide consistency and a sharper focus so that the Gospel readings would underscore the most appropriate concept(s) for each season.

Lent prior to the Council had focused overwhelmingly on penitence; the new Lectionary now brings forward in addition the more ancient sense of Lent as a preparation for Easter—for the Baptism of the elect in the catechumenate (called the period of purification and enlightenment) and also for the renewal of baptismal promises for the baptized, who relive and deepen their own Baptisms by supporting those preparing for initiation. Now readings are given in Year A to accompany the "scrutinies" on the Third, Fourth, and Fifth Sundays in Lent (the rites through which the community prays intently for those preparing for Baptism—for the removal of sin or any other barriers to their initiation). Those particularly powerful

---

6   In Rome, from the fourth century, three days (Wednesday, Friday, and Saturday) were set aside for fasting in Advent during the complete week before Christmas Eve and after the commemoration of St. Lucy. Intended as preparation for Christmas, similar ember days of preparation were designated before Lent, Pentecost, and the Exaltation of the Holy Cross, and the practice spread to other regions.

readings may be read on these Sundays in any year, whenever the elect are present. The original intent of the compilers was to use the same readings for Lent every year. The bishops, however, recommended the addition of different readings for Years B and C. Now the readings provided for Years B and C tend to concern God's mercy inviting us to repentance and conversion.

During Ordinary Time the Gospel readings, generally from the synoptic Gospel of the year, follow the order in which they are found in their canonical text, although most do not pick up exactly where the last reading left off on the previous Sunday. Passages that would be used on solemnities or during the liturgical seasons of Advent, Christmas Time, Lent, and Easter Time are skipped over. During Ordinary Time, stories that occur in all three synoptic accounts are rarely matched across the three years: Matthew's story of Jesus at first refusing and then healing the daughter of the Canaanite woman, whose wit and wisdom cause Jesus to change his mind (Matthew 15:21–28), is assigned to the Twentieth Sunday of Year A, but the similar account featuring a Syrophoenician woman in Mark 7:24–30 does not appear in the Sunday Lectionary.

In the liturgical seasons and on particular feasts, however, some parallel passages considered to be especially important are assigned every year to the same Sunday on the calendar, which means that each year on a particular Sunday we will be contemplating the same story or teaching from a different evangelist (Matthew, Mark, or Luke). Thus, on the First Sunday of Advent, the Gospel Reading is taken from Jesus' teaching about the end times found in the synoptic Gospel for that year. We hear John the Baptist preaching during each year for the next two Sundays of Advent. On the First Sunday of Lent, the account of Jesus' temptations is assigned from the synoptic Gospel of the year. Then, on the Second Sunday of Lent, the account of the Transfiguration is assigned from that year's synoptic Gospel. We hear the Passion reading on Palm Sunday from each evangelist in the appropriate year, and the discovery of the empty tomb at the Easter Vigil.[7] Other parallel accounts are introduced each year but on different Sundays. The story of Jesus' miraculous feeding is a good example. Matthew 14:13–21 is assigned to the Eighteenth Sunday of Year A. Mark's account of what leads up to this miracle from Mark 6:30–34 is assigned to the Sixteenth Sunday of Year B, followed by John's account of the feeding from John 6:1–15 on the Seventeenth Sunday of Year B. In Year C, the compilers thought it most appropriate to place Luke's story of the miraculous feeding on the Solemnity of the Most Holy Body and Blood of Christ.[8] In each of the three years there is a distinct plan for the lessons we will hear from the Gospel accounts. Where, in the judgment of the compilers, the liturgical year calls for it, all three accounts will speak in one voice.

Three Readings for Each Sunday

Another major decision was to include three readings for the Sunday Lectionary. (Rome had followed a three-reading pattern until the fifth century.) It was also determined that, excepting the Sundays of Easter, when the First Reading would be from the Acts of the Apostles, all First Readings would come from the Old Testament.[9] With a few exceptions, the Second Reading would come from an Epistle.[10]

The three readings were set in sequence punctuated by ritual music. The First Reading would be followed by a psalm or canticle, the refrain sung by the congregation and the verses sung by a psalmist

---

7 Bonneau, 38.

8 Traditionally this observance is called Corpus Christi and is celebrated on the Thursday after Trinity Sunday. In the United States it is observed on the Sunday following Trinity Sunday and the readings for this observance replace those assigned to that Sunday in Ordinary Time.

9 It was also determined that national bishops conferences might choose to allow for the use of only two readings. This was helpful for some regions where a complete translation of the Old Testament did not exist.

10 A passage from Acts of the Apostles is the Second Reading for the observance of the Baptism of the Lord in Year B. Selections from the Book of Revelation are appointed as the Second Readings for the Sundays of Easter in Year C.

Table 2

Three-Year Cycle of Readings for Sundays and Some Solemnities of Advent, Christmas Time, Lent, Easter Time, and Ordinary Time

Sunday, Solemnity, or Feast			
Advent	**Year A**	**Year B**	**Year C**
First Sunday of Advent	Isaiah 2:1–5 Romans 13:11–14 Matthew 24:37–44	Isaiah 63:16b–17, 19b; 64:2–7 1 Corinthians 1:3–9 Mark 13:33–37	Jeremiah 33:14–16 1 Thessalonians 3:12—4:2 Luke 21:25–28, 34–36
Second Sunday of Advent	Isaiah 11:1–10 Romans 15:4–9 Matthew 3:1–12	Isaiah 40:1–5, 9–11 2 Peter 3:8–14 Mark 1:1–8	Baruch 5:1–9 Philippians 1:4–6, 8–11 Luke 3:1–6
Third Sunday of Advent	Isaiah 35:1–6a, 10 James 5:7–10 Matthew 11:2–11	Isaiah 61:1–2a, 10–11 1 Thessalonians 5:16–24 John 1:6–8, 19–28	Zephaniah 3:14a–18a Philippians 4:4–7 Luke 3:10–18
Fourth Sunday of Advent	Isaiah 7:10–14 Romans 1:1–7 Matthew 1:18–24	2 Samuel 7:1–5, 8b–12, 14a, 16 Romans 16:25–27 Luke 1:26–38	Micah 5:1–4a Hebrews 10:5–10 Luke 1:39–45
Christmas Time	**Year A**	**Year B**	**Year C**
Nativity of the Lord: Vigil A, B, C	Isaiah 62:1–5 Acts 13:16–17, 22–25 Matthew 1:1–25 [18–25]		
Nativity of the Lord: Night A, B, C	Isaiah 9:1–6 Titus 2:11–14 Luke 2:1–14		
Nativity of the Lord: Dawn A, B, C	Isaiah 62:11–12 Titus 3:4–7 Luke 2:15–20		
Nativity of the Lord: Day A, B, C	Isaiah 52:7–10 Hebrews 1:1–6 John 1:1–18 [1–5, 9–14]		
Holy Family of Jesus, Mary, and Joseph	Sirach 3:2–6, 12–14 Colossians 3:12–21 Matthew 2:13–15, 19–23	Genesis 15:1–6; 21:1–3 Hebrews 11:8, 11–12, 17–19 Luke 2:22–40 [22, 39–40]	1 Samuel 1:20–22, 24–28 1 John 3:1–2, 21–24 Luke 2:41–52

Sunday, Solemnity, or Feast			
Christmas Time	**Year A**	**Year B**	**Year C**
Mary, the Holy Mother of God A, B, C	Numbers 6:22–27 Galatians 4:4–7 Luke 2:16–21		
Second Sunday after Christmas A, B, C	Sirach 24:1–2, 8–12 Ephesians 1:3–6, 15–18 John 1:1–18 [1–5, 9–14]		
Epiphany of the Lord A, B, C	Isaiah 60:1–6 Ephesians 3:2–3a, 5–6 Matthew 2:1–12		
Baptism of the Lord	Isaiah 42:1–4, 6–7 Acts 10:34–38 Matthew 3:13–17	Isaiah 55:1–11 1 John 5:1–9 Mark 1:7–11	Isaiah 40:1–5, 9–11 Titus 2:11–14, 3:4–7 Luke 3:15–16, 21–22
Lent	**Year A**	**Year B**	**Year C**
First Sunday of Lent	Genesis 2:7–9; 3:1–7 Romans 5:12–19 [5:12, 17–19] Matthew 4:1–11	Genesis 9:8–15 1 Peter 3:18–22 Mark 1:12–15	Deuteronomy 26:4–10 Romans 10:8–13 Luke 4:1–13
Second Sunday of Lent	Genesis 12:1–4a 2 Timothy 1:8b–10 Matthew 17:1–9	Genesis 22:1–2, 9a, 10–13, 15–18 Romans 8:31b–34 Mark 9:2–10	Genesis 15:5–12, 17–18 Philippians 3:17—4:1 [3:20—4:1] Luke 9:28b–36
Third Sunday of Lent	Exodus 17:3–7 Romans 5:1–2, 5–8 John 4:5–42 [4:5–15, 19b–26, 39a, 40–42]	Exodus 20:1–17 [20:1–3, 7–8, 12–17] 1 Corinthians 1:22–25 John 2:13–25	Exodus 3:1–8a, 13–15 1 Corinthians 10:1–6, 10–12 Luke 13:1–9
Fourth Sunday of Lent	1 Samuel 16:1b, 6–7, 10–13a Ephesians 5:8–14 John 9:1–41 [9:1, 6–9, 13–17, 34–38]	2 Chronicles 36:14–16, 19–23 Ephesians 2:4–10 John 3:14–21	Joshua 5:9a, 10–12 2 Corinthians 5:17–21 Luke 15:1–3, 11–32
Fifth Sunday of Lent	Ezekiel 37:12–14 Romans 8:8–11 John 11:1–45 [11:3–7, 17, 20–27, 33b–45]	Jeremiah 31:31–34 Hebrews 5:7–9 John 12:20–33	Isaiah 43:16–21 Philippians 3:8–14 John 8:1–11

Lent	Year A	Year B	Year C
Palm Sunday of the Lord's Passion	A: Matthew 21:1–11 A, B, C: Isaiah 50:4–7 A, B, C: Philippians 2:6–11 A: Matthew 26:14—27:66 [27:11–54]	B: Mark 11:1–10 B: Mark 14:1—15:47 [15:1–39]	C: Luke 19:28–40 C: Luke 22:14—23:56 [23:1–49]
Holy Thursday: Mass of the Lord's Supper A, B, C	Exodus 12:1–8, 11–14 1 Corinthians 11:23–26 John 13:1–15		
Good Friday of the Lord's Passion A, B, C	Isaiah 52:13—53:12 Hebrews 4:14–16; 5:7–9 John 18:1—19:42		
Easter Vigil A, B, C	Genesis 1:1—2:2 [1:1, 26–31a] Genesis 22:1–18 [22:1–2, 9a , 10–13, 15–18] Exodus 14:15—15:1 Isaiah 54:5 –14 Isaiah 55:1–11 Baruch 3:9–15, 32–4:4 Ezekiel 36:16–17a, 18–28 Romans 6:3–11 A: Matthew 28:1–10	B: Mark 16:1–7	C: Luke 24:1–12

Easter Time	Year A	Year B	Year C
Easter Sunday A, B, C	Acts 10:34a, 37–43 Colossians 3:1–4 OR 1 Corinthians 5:6b–8 John 20:1–9 OR A: Matthew 28:1–10 (fr. Easter Vigil) Afternoon Gospel: Luke 24:13–35	OR B: Mark 16:1–7 (fr. Easter Vigil)	OR C: Luke 24:1–12 (fr. Easter Vigil)

Easter Time	Year A	Year B	Year C
Second Sunday of Easter	Acts 2:42–47 1 Peter 1:3–9 John 20:19–31	Acts 4:32–35 1 John 5:1–6 John 20:19–31	Acts 5:12–16 Revelation 1:9–11a, 12–13, 17–19 John 20:19–31
Third Sunday of Easter	Acts 2:14, 22–33 1 Peter 1:17–21 Luke 24:13–35	Acts 3:13–15, 17–19 1 John 2:1–5a Luke 24:35–48	Acts 5:27–32, 40b–41 Revelation 5:11–14 John 21:1–19 [21:1–14]
Fourth Sunday of Easter	Acts 2:14a, 36–41 1 Peter 2:20b–25 John 10:1–10	Acts 4:8–12 1 John 3:1–2 John 10:11–18	Acts 13:14, 43–52 Revelation 7:9, 14b–17 John 10:27–30
Fifth Sunday of Easter	Acts 6:1–7 1 Peter 2:4–9 John 14:1–12	Acts 9:26–31 1 John 3:18–24 John 15:1–8	Acts 14:21–27 Revelation 21:1–5a John 13:31–33a, 34–35
Sixth Sunday of Easter	Acts 8:5–8, 14–17 1 Peter 3:15–18 John 14:15–21	Acts 10:25–26, 34–35, 44–48 1 John 4:7–10 John 15:9–17	Acts 15:1–2, 22–29 Revelation 21:10–14, 22–23 John 14:23–29
Ascension of the Lord	Acts 1:1–11 Ephesians 1:17–23 Matthew 28:16–20	Acts 1:1–11 Ephesians 4:1–13 [4:1–7, 11–13] Mark 16:15–20	Acts 1:1–11 Ephesians 1:17–23 or Hebrews 9:24–28; 10:19–23 Luke 24:46–53
Seventh Sunday of Easter	Acts 1:12–14 1 Peter 4:13–16 John 17:1–11a	Acts 1:15 –17, 20a, 20c–26 1 John 4:11–16 John 17:11b–19	Acts 7:55–60 Revelation 22:12–14, 16–17, 20 John 17:20–26
Pentecost Sunday	Acts 2:1–11 1 Corinthians 12:3b–7, 12–13 John 20:19–23	Acts 2:1–11 Galatians 5:16–25 John 15:26–27; 16:12–15	Acts 2:1–11 Romans 8:8–17 or 1 Corinthians 12:3b–7, 12–13 John 14:15–16, 23b–26

Ordinary Time	Year A	Year B	Year C
The Most Holy Trinity	Exodus 34:4b–6, 8 –9 2 Corinthians 13:11–13 John 3:16–18	Deuteronomy 4:32–34, 39–40 Romans 8:14–17 Matthew 28:16–20	Proverbs 8:22–31 Romans 5:1–5 John 16:12–15

Ordinary Time	Year A	Year B	Year C
The Most Holy Body and Blood of Christ	Deuteronomy 8:2–4, 14b–16a 1 Corinthians 10:16–17 John 6:51–58	Exodus 24:3–8 Hebrews 9:11–15 Mark 14:12–16, 22–26	Genesis 14:18–20 1 Corinthians 11:23–26 Luke 9:11b–17
Second Sunday in Ordinary Time	Isaiah 49:3, 5–6 1 Corinthians 1:1–3 John 1:29–34	1 Samuel 3:3b–10, 19 1 Corinthians 6:13c–15a, 17–20 John 1:35–42	Isaiah 62:1–5 1 Corinthians 12:4–11 John 2:1–11
Third Sunday in Ordinary Time	Isaiah 8:23—9:3 1 Corinthians 1:10–13, 17 Matthew 4:12–23 [4:12–17]	Jonah 3:1–5, 10 1 Corinthians 7:29–31 Mark 1:14–20	Nehemiah 8:2–4a, 5–6, 8–10 1 Corinthians 12:12–30 [12:12–14, 27] Luke 1:1–4; 4:14–21
Fourth Sunday in Ordinary Time	Zephaniah 2:3; 3:12–13 1 Corinthians 1:26–31 Matthew 5:1–12a	Deuteronomy 18:15–20 1 Corinthians 7:32–35 Mark 1:21–28	Jeremiah 1:4–5, 17–19 1 Corinthians 12:31—13:13 [13:4–13] Luke 4:21–30
Fifth Sunday in Ordinary Time	Isaiah 58:7–10 1 Corinthians 2:1–5 Matthew 5:13–16	Job 7:1–4, 6–7 1 Corinthians 9:16–19, 22–23 Mark 1:29–39	Isaiah 6:1–2a, 3–8 1 Corinthians 15:1–11 [15:3–8, 11] Luke 5:1–11
Sixth Sunday in Ordinary Time	Sirach 15:15–20 1 Corinthians 2:6–10 Matthew 5:17–37 [4:20–22a, 27–28, 33–34a, 37]	Leviticus 13:1–2, 44–46 1 Corinthians 10:31—11:1 Mark 1:40–45	Jeremiah 17:5–8 1 Corinthians 15:12, 16–20 Luke 6:17, 20–26
Seventh Sunday in Ordinary Time	Leviticus 19:1–2, 17–18 1 Corinthians 3:16–23 Matthew 5:38–48	Isaiah 43:18–19, 21–22, 24b–25 2 Corinthians 1:18–22 Mark 2:1–12	1 Samuel 26:2, 7–9, 12–13, 22–23 1 Corinthians 15:45–49 Luke 6:27–38
Eighth Sunday in Ordinary Time	Isaiah 49:14–15 Psalm 62:2–3, 6–7, 8–9 (6a) 1 Corinthians 4:1–5 Matthew 6:24–34	Hosea 2:16b, 21–22 2 Corinthians 3:1b–6 Mark 2:18–22	Sirach 27:4–7 1 Corinthians 15:54–58 Luke 6:39–45

Sunday, Solemnity, or Feast			
Ordinary Time	**Year A**	**Year B**	**Year C**
Ninth Sunday in Ordinary Time	Deuteronomy 11:18, 26–28, 32 Romans 3:21–25, 28 Matthew 7:21–27	Deuteronomy 5:12–15 2 Corinthians 4:6–11 Mark 2:23—3:6	1 Kings 8:41–43 Galatians 1:1–2, 6–10 Luke 7: –10
Tenth Sunday in Ordinary Time	Deuteronomy 11:18, 26 –28, 32 Romans 3:21–25a, 28 Matthew 9:9–13	Genesis 3:9–15 2 Corinthians 4:13—5:1 Mark 3:20–35	1 Kings 17:17–24 Galatians 1:11–19 Luke 7:11–17
Eleventh Sunday in Ordinary Time	Exodus 19:2–6a Romans 5:6–11 Matthew 9:36—10:8	Ezekiel 17:22 –24 2 Corinthians 5:6–10 Mark 4:26–34	2 Samuel 12:7–10 Galatians 2:16, 19–21 Luke 7:36—8:3 [7:36–50]
Twelfth Sunday in Ordinary Time	Jeremiah 20:10–13 Romans 5:12–15 Matthew 10:26–33	Job 38:1, 8–11 2 Corinthians 5:14–17 Mark 4:35–41	Zechariah 12:10–11;13:1 Galatians 3:26–29 Luke 9:18–25
Thirteenth Sunday in Ordinary Time	2 Kings 4:8–11, 14–16a Romans 6:3–4, 8–11 Matthew 10:37–42	Wisdom 1:13–15; 2:23–24 2 Corinthians 8:7, 9, 13–15 Mark 5:21–43 [5:21–24, 35b–43]	1 Kings 19:16b, 19–21 Galatians 5:1, 13–18 Luke 9:51–62
Fourteenth Sunday in Ordinary Time	Zechariah 9:9–10 Romans 8:9, 11–13 Matthew 11:25–30	Ezekiel 2:2–5 2 Corinthians 12:7–10 Mark 6:1–6	Isaiah 66:10–14c Galaltians 6:14–18 Luke 10:1–12, 17–20 [10:1–9]
Fifteenth Sunday in Ordinary Time	Isaiah 55:10–11 Romans 8:18–23 Matthew 13:1–23 [13:1–9]	Amos 7:12–15 Ephesians 1:3–14 [1:3–10] Mark 6:7–13	Deuteronomy 30:10–14 Colossians 1:15–20 Luke 10:25–37
Sixteenth Sunday in Ordinary Time	Wisdom 12:13, 16–19 Romans 8:26–27 Matthew 13:24–43 [13:24–39]	Jeremiah 23:1–6 Ephesians 2:13–18 Mark 6:30–34	Genesis 18:1–10a Colossians 1:24–28 Luke 10:38–42
Seventeenth Sunday in Ordinary Time	1 Kings 3:5, 7–12 Romans 8:28–30 Matthew 13:44–52 [13:44–46]	2 Kings 4:42–44 Ephesians 4:1–6 John 6:1–15	Genesis 18:20–32 Colossians 2:12–14 Luke 11:1–13

Sunday, Solemnity, or Feast	Year A	Year B	Year C
Eighteenth Sunday in Ordinary Time	Isaiah 55:1–3 Romans 8:35, 37–39 Matthew 14:13–21	Exodus 16:2–4, 12–15 Ephesians 4:17, 20–24 John 6:24–35	Ecclesiastes 1:2; 2:21–23 Colossians 3:1–5, 9–11 Luke 12:13–21
Nineteenth Sunday in Ordinary Time	1 Kings 19:9a, 11–13a Romans 9:1–5 Matthew 14:22–33	1 Kings 19:4–8 Ephesians 4:30—5:2 John 6:41–51	Wisdom 18:6–9 Hebrews 11:1–2, 8–19 [11:1–2, 8–12] Luke 12:32–48 [12:35–40]
Twentieth Sunday in Ordinary Time	Isaiah 56:1, 6–7 Romans 11:13–15, 29–32 Matthew 15:21–28	Proverbs 9:1–6 Ephesians 5:15–20 John 6:51–58	Jeremiah 38:4–6, 8–10 Hebrews 12:1–4 Luke 12:49–53
Twenty-First Sunday in Ordinary Time	Isaiah 22:19–23 Romans 11:33–36 Matthew 16:13–20	Joshua 24:1–2a, 15–17, 18b Ephesians 5:21–32 [5:2a, 25–32] John 6:60–69	Isaiah 66:18–21 Hebrews 12:5–7, 11–13 Luke 13:22–30
Twenty-Second Sunday in Ordinary Time	Jeremiah 20:7–9 Romans 12:1–2 Matthew 16:21–27	Deuteronomy 4:1–2, 6–8 James 1:17–18, 21b–22, 27 Mark 7:1–8, 14–15, 21–23	Sirach 3:17–18, 20, 28–29 Hebrews 12:18–19, 22–24a Luke 14:1, 7–14
Twenty-Third Sunday in Ordinary Time	Ezekiel 33:7–9 Romans 13:8–10 Matthew 18:15–20	Isaiah 35:4–7a James 2:1–5 Mark 7:31–37	Wisdom 9:13–18b Philemon 9–10, 12–17 Luke 14:25–33
Twenty-Fourth Sunday in Ordinary Time	Sirach 27:30—28:7 Romans 14:7–9 Matthew 18:21–35	Isaiah 50:5–9a James 2:14–18 Mark 8:27–35	Exodus 32:7–11, 13–14 1 Timothy 1:12–17 Luke 15:1–32 [15:1–10]
Twenty-Fifth Sunday in Ordinary Time	Isaiah 55:6–9 Philippians 1:20c–24, 27a Matthew 20:1–16a	Wisdom 2:12, 17–20 James 3:16—4:3 Mark 9:30–37	Amos 8:4–7 1 Timothy 2:1–8 Luke 16:1–13 [16:10–13]

Sunday, Solemnity, or Feast	Year A	Year B	Year C
Twenty-Sixth Sunday in Ordinary Time	Ezekiel 18:25–28 Philippians 2:1–11 [2:1–5] Matthew 21:28–32	Numbers 11:25–29 James 5:1–6 Mark 9:38–43, 45, 47–48	Amos 6:1a, 4–7 1 Timothy 6:11–16 Luke 16:19–31
Twenty-Seventh Sunday in Ordinary Time	Isaiah 5:1–7 Philippians 4:6–9 Matthew 21:33–43	Genesis 2:18–24 Hebrews 2:9–11 Mark 10:2–16 [10:2–12]	Habakkuk 1:2–3; 2:2–4 2 Timothy 1:6–8, 13–14 Luke 17:5–10
Twenty-Eighth Sunday in Ordinary Time	Isaiah 25:6–10a Philippians 4:12–14, 19–20 Matthew 22:1–14 [22:1–10]	Wisdom 7:7–11 Hebrews 4:12–13 Mark 10:17–30 [10:17–27]	2 Kings 5:14–17 2 Timothy 2:8–13 Luke 17:11–19
Twenty-Ninth Sunday in Ordinary Time	Isaiah 45:1, 4–6 1 Thessalonians 1:1–5b Matthew 22:15–21	Isaiah 53:10–11 Hebrews 4:14–16 Mark 10:35–45 [10:42–45]	Exodus 17:8–13 2 Timothy 3:14–4:2 Luke 18:1–8
Thirtieth Sunday in Ordinary Time	Exodus 22:20–26 1 Thessalonians 1:5c–10 Matthew 22:34–40	Jeremiah 31:7–9 Hebrews 5:1–6 Mark 10:46–52	Sirach 35:12–14, 16–18 2 Timothy 4:6–8, 16–18 Luke 18:9–14
Thirty-First Sunday in Ordinary Time	Malachi 1:14b–2:2b, 8–10 1 Thessalonians 2:7b–9, 13	Deuteronomy 6:2–6 Hebrews 7:23–28 Mark 12:28b–34	Wisdom 11:22—12:2 2 Thessalonians 1:11—2:2 Luke 19:1–10
Thirty-Second Sunday in Ordinary Time	Wisdom 6:12–16 1 Thessalonians 4:13–18 [4:13–14] Matthew 25:1–13	1 Kings 17:10–16 Hebrews 9:24–28 Mark 12:38–44 [12:41–44]	2 Maccabees 7:1–2, 9–14 2 Thessalonians 2:16–3:5 Luke 20:27–38 [20:27, 34–38]

or choir. The Gospel selection, which constituted the final reading, would be preceded by a sung dialogue between cantor (or choir) and congregation. First, alleluias would be sung by the cantor or choir and repeated by the congregation; then a verse from the Bible related to the message of the Gospel would be sung by choir or cantor, followed by a second acclamation of alleluias from the congregation. During Lent, the alleluias are replaced by singing "Glory and Praise to You, Lord Jesus Christ,"[11] followed by a verse from a Gospel. This arrangement is called "The Verse before the Gospel." For the rest of the year the Lectionary identifies this verse as the "Alleluia Verse."

The relationships among the readings, as the Introduction to the Lectionary makes clear, were determined by one of two principles: "harmony" or "semicontinuity."[12] Gospel Readings during Ordinary Time (as well as those of the Epistles to be noted below), are semicontinuous passages that follow the sequence in the Gospel but often skip over stories in the canonical text. Harmony operates between the Old Testament and New Testament readings when the events and themes described in each are closely related. During Ordinary Time, the Old Testament texts are usually chosen to harmonize with the New, whereas during Advent, Lent, and Easter Time, the texts are chosen to illuminate the themes of the seasons.

The First Readings

Apart from the fifty days of Easter Time, the First Readings are from Old Testament, and, as explained, largely chosen to correspond to the Gospel. In many instances the harmony between the two follows an approach to Scripture called "typology," in which Christian readers see people, events, or images in the Old Testament as "types"— patterns or symbols—of those in the Gospel. In this parallel relationship between the two, the Old Testament type prefigures what will unfold later in salvation history through Jesus Christ. For example,

---

11 Or another similar verse such as "Praise to you, Lord Jesus Christ, King of endless glory!"

12 Introduction to the Lectionary, 66.3–67.

in the reading for the Third Sunday of Lent, Year A, the story of Moses striking the rock so that God can cause water to flow out for the untrusting people to drink is a type of the encounter in that day's Gospel between the woman of Samaria and Jesus, who will offer her living water and initiate her conversion. In this way the compilers wished to show "that the entire Old Testament is presupposed in the Lord's preaching, his actions, and his passion."[13]

During Ordinary Time, sometimes the linkage between First Reading and Gospel is not as straightforward. For example, on the Fifth Sunday in Ordinary Time, Year B, their relationship is one of contrast. Job's hopelessness (Job 4:1–4, 6–7) is the opposite of Christ's active life of healing and teaching (Mark 1:29–39). In other instances the relationship seems to rest on the use of a similar word or general topic. For example on the Thirty-Third Sunday in Ordinary Time, Year A, the reading from Proverbs (31:10–13, 19–20, 30–31) about the "worthy wife" is paired with Jesus' parable from Matthew (25:14–30) about three servants who were given talents by their master. Both texts advise about the wise management of resources, but in different ways.

During Advent, Christmas Time, Lent, and on solemnities and major feasts, the three readings harmonize well around the event or themes celebrated. Advent's First Readings are prophecies about the coming of a messiah, mostly from Isaiah, that allude to the Savior who is anticipated in the Gospel Readings. During Lent, (outside of the Third, Fourth, and Fifth Sundays of Year A) the First and Second Readings better correspond to each other, more than either does to the Gospel Reading. For example, on the Second Sunday of Lent in Year B the First Reading from Genesis recounts how God instructed Abraham to sacrifice his son, and yet, since Abraham did not withhold his beloved son, God provided a ram for the sacrifice (Genesis 22:1–2, 92, 10–13, 15–18). The Second Reading from Romans states that "God is for us" since "he . . . did not spare his own Son to die"

---

13 Bugnini, 411.

(Romans 8:31–34). While there are ways to see how these two readings can be linked with Mark's account of the Transfiguration (9:2–10), they correspond much more closely with each other than they do with the Gospel selection.

The Responsorial Psalm

Between the First Reading and Second Reading, the Sunday Lectionary provides a Responsorial Psalm taken from the psalms, canticles, or one of the other books in the Bible. This selection is designed to be sung by the whole community, by a psalmist alone, or ideally in a responsorial form in which a cantor sings the text and the assembly sings the refrain. The least-favored alternative is for the psalm to be proclaimed by a reader, with the community speaking the response.

Each Responsorial Psalm chosen relates to at least one other reading for the day in one of several ways: (1) It is cited or alluded to directly in one of the other readings. (2) It reinforces an idea from the First Reading. (3) It is considered suitable to the occasion.

For some occasions, the text used for the Responsorial Psalm comes from one of the biblical canticles. For example, on the Third Sunday of Advent in Year B, a portion of the *Magnificat* (Luke 1:46–50, 53–54), Mary's response to Elizabeth's prophecy of her blessedness and favor with the Lord, is used for the Responsorial Psalm.

For every season and for Ordinary Time, the Lectionary provides a few psalm options that can be used throughout the entire season. The compilers sensed that the use of one Responsorial Psalm over an extended period could unify the season, and they also wanted to make it easier for parishes to sing the Responsorial Psalm by eliminating the need to learn new music each week. The psalm or canticle is "an integral part of the liturgy of the Word."[14] In it, the worshiping assembly turns from attentive listening to communal prayer and affirmation. The faithful come to "perceive the word of God speaking in the psalms and to turn these psalms into the prayer of the

---

14 *General Instruction of the Roman Missal,* 61.

Church."[15] In this way, the Responsorial Psalm pertains as much to the liturgy and music, as it does to Scripture.

The Second Readings

During the liturgical seasons of Advent, Christmas Time, and Lent, and for all Solemnities, the Second Readings were selected to connect thematically to the other readings for that day and to the spirit of the season. During Advent and Christmas Time the connection between the Second Reading and the Gospel is fairly prominent, but, as mentioned above, during Lent there is a stronger connection between the First and Second Reading than between either of those readings and the Gospel for the day. The Second Readings for the Sundays in Easter Time follow three ancient traditions. In Year A these semicontinuous selections move through 1 Peter; in Year B, they move through 1 John; and in Year C they move through the Book of Revelation. Most have little connection to the other readings.

In Ordinary Time, the selections from a letter follow a three-year plan (for Years A, B, and C), shown in Table 3 at the end of this section. Excerpts from thirteen New Testament letters are spread across the Sundays, allowing us to hear semicontinuous reading of twelve of them. (Exceptions to this pattern include a single excerpt from the Letter to Philemon, on the Twenty-Third Sunday of Year C, and the Second Reading for the last Sunday of the Year, the Solemnity of Our Lord Jesus Christ, King of the Universe.) The selections do not pick up exactly where the last reading ended, but they provide a fairly sustained reading of a good portion of the twelve letters. While, as noted above, semicontinuous readings from the Acts of the Apostles are assigned as the First Reading from Easter Time to Pentecost, a selection from Acts is assigned as the Second Reading for the Feast of the Baptism of the Lord in Year A.

---

15 Introduction to the Lectionary, 19.

Table 3

Sunday Second Readings, Ordinary Time

Sunday	Year A	Year B	Year C
2	1 Corinthians 1:1–3	1 Corinthians 6:13c–15a, 17–20	1 Corinthians 12:4–11
3	1 Corinthians 1:10–13, 17	1 Corinthians 7:29–31	1 Corinthians 12:12–30 or 12:12–14, 27
4	1 Corinthians 1:26–31	1 Corinthians 7:32–35	1 Corinthians 12:31—13:13 or 13:4–13
5	1 Corinthians 2:1–5	1 Corinthians 9:16–19, 22–23	1 Corinthians 15:1–11 or 15:3–8, 11
6	1 Corinthians 2:6–10	1 Corinthians 10:31—11:1	1 Corinthians 15:12, 16–20
7	1 Corinthians 3:16–23	2 Corinthians 1:18–22	1 Corinthians 15:45–49
8	1 Corinthians 4:1–5	2 Corinthians 3:1b–6	1 Corinthians 15:54–58
9	Romans 3:21–25, 28	2 Corinthians 4:6–11	Galatians 1:1–2, 6–10
10	Romans 4:18–25	2 Corinthians 4:13—5:1	Galatians 1:11–19
11	Romans 5:6–11	2 Corinthians 5:6–10	Galatians 2:16, 19–21
12	Romans 5:12–15	2 Corinthians 5:14–17	Galatians 3:26–29
13	Romans 6:3–4, 8–11	2 Corinthians 8:7, 9, 13–15	Galatians 5:1, 13–18
14	Romans 8:9, 11–13	2 Corinthians 12:7–10	Galatians 6:14–18
15	Romans 8:18–23	Ephesians 1:3–14 or 1:3–10	Colossians 1:15–20
16	Romans 8:26–27	Ephesians 2:13–18	Colossians 1:24–28
17	Romans 8:28–30	Ephesians 4:1–6	Colossians 2:12–14
18	Romans 8:35, 37–39	Ephesians 4:17, 20–24	Colossians 3:1–5, 9–11
19	Romans 9:1–5	Ephesians 4:30—5:2	Hebrews 11:1–2, 8–19 or 11:1–2, 8–12
20	Romans 11:13–15, 29–32	Ephesians 5:15–20	Hebrews 12:1–4
21	Romans 11:33–36	Ephesians 5:21–32 or 5:2a, 25–32	Hebrews 12:5–7, 11–13
22	Romans 12:1–2	James 1:17–18, 21b–22, 27	Hebrews 12:18–19, 22–24a
23	Romans 13:8–10	James 2:1–5	Philemon 9–10, 12–17
24	Romans 14:7–9	James 2:14–18	1 Timothy 1:12–17
25	Philippians 1:20c–24, 27a	James 3:16—4:3	1 Timothy 2:1–8
26	Philippians 2:1–11 or 2:1–5	James 5:1–6	1 Timothy 6:11–16
27	Philippians 4:6–9	Hebrews 2:9–11	2 Timothy 1:6–8, 13–14

28	Philippians 4:12–14, 19–20	Hebrews 4:12–13	2 Timothy 2:8–13
29	1 Thessalonians 1:1–5b	Hebrews 4:14–16	2 Timothy 3:14—4:2
30	1 Thessalonians 1:5c–10	Hebrews 5:1–6	2 Timothy 4:6–8, 16–18
31	1 Thessalonians 2:7b–9, 13	Hebrews 7:23–28	2 Thessalonians 1:11—2:2
32	1 Thessalonians 4: 13–18 or 1:13–14	Hebrews 9:24–28	2 Thessalonians 2:16—3:5
33	1 Thessalonians 5:1–6	Hebrews 10:11–14, 18	2 Thessalonians 3:7–12
34	1 Corinthians 15:20–26, 28	Revelation 1:5–8	Colossians 1:12–20

A Two-Year Weekday Lectionary

The weekday Lectionary enriches those who attend daily Mass with many passages that were not included in the Sunday readings. This Lectionary assigns two readings to each Mass with a Responsorial Psalm between the First Reading and the Gospel. Although it is called a two-year Lectionary and identifies odd-numbered years (for example, 2015) as Year I and even-numbered years (such as 2016) as Year II, only the First Readings and Responsorial Psalms for Ordinary Time differ. The readings for the liturgical seasons are identical for both years and the Gospel Readings for weekdays of Ordinary Time are the same every year.

The weekday selections, like those for Sundays and solemnities, emphasize the themes of each season: anticipation for Advent, celebration of the Incarnation during Christmas Time, penitence and Baptism during Lent. The Gospel Readings during Lent, in addition to teaching the lessons of the season, provide semicontinuous reading of John, chapters 4–13, from the fourth week on. Throughout Easter Time, the First Readings for weekdays are from the Acts of the Apostles, as they are on Sundays. The Gospel Readings, after presenting the accounts of Christ's Resurrection and encounters with the Risen Christ in the octave of Easter, turn to a long series of semicontinuous selections from John 3–17, and end the season with the last verses of John's account.

Weekdays in Ordinary Time provide semicontinuous passages from the synoptic Gospels: Mark 1–12 in weeks 1–9; Matthew 5–25 in weeks 10–21; Luke 4–21 in weeks 22–34, ending with Luke's account of Jesus' eschatological discourse. First Readings during Ordinary Time are different in the Year I and Year II cycles, so they add greatly to the range of Scripture presented to the faithful. They come from both the Old and New Testaments, usually presented as a series of weeks from one Testament before switching to the other. Some weeks feature a single book, but in others, one or two selections from multiple books are included. In a two-year period, only Obadiah, Zephaniah, and the Song of Songs are not included in at least one weekday selection, so over that two-year period, daily Mass attendees hear a representative passage from almost every book of the Bible.

Readings for Celebrating the Saints

Like the revision of the Lectionary, the revision of the General Roman Calendar[16] responded to guidelines set out in the Second Vatican Council's *Constitution on the Sacred Liturgy*. While affirming the veneration of the saints, whose feasts "proclaim the wonderful works of Christ in his servants," the Council fathers stressed that their feasts should not "take precedence over the feasts commemorating the very mysteries of salvation."[17] That was precisely the problem with the calendar that the Council recognized it needed to address.[18]

Principles governing the revision included: (1) Decreasing the number of saints' days on the General Roman Calendar. (This was

---

16 The revision resulted in *Universal Norms on the Liturgical Year and the General Roman Calendar*, published in 1969.

17 SC, 11.

18 Adolf Adam points out that in 1950, 272 of the 365 days of the year were assigned feasts of saints, which certainly obscured the celebration of the seasons and times through which the faithful enter into the mysteries of salvation history. *The Liturgical Year, Its History and Its Meaning after the Reform of the Liturgy* (Collegeville, MN: Liturgical Press, 1990), 209.

accomplished by shifting those not universally significant from the general calendar to the calendars of local regions and by removing some saints from the calendar whose lives could not be historically verified.[19]) (2) Ranking all the commemorations in order of importance: solemnities, feasts, obligatory memorials, and optional memorials. (3) Placing the observance of the saint on the day he or she entered eternal life. (4) Ensuring that the General Roman Calendar was more representative of historical periods, geographical areas, and cultures.[20]

The new Lectionary had a role to play in providing more focus in the celebration of the saints.[21] The most important people were given solemnities (Mary, Joseph, John the Baptist, and the Apostles Peter and Paul). Feasts were assigned to Mary, the remaining Apostles and evangelists, a few martyrs, and the archangels. Memorials were designated to celebrate saints who appear in the New Testament and were held in special esteem by the entire Church. Optional memorials were given to other saints. Much care was given to assembling texts that would highlight truly significant aspects of a saint's life or character. If Scripture readings specifically about the saint existed, those were assigned to the day of the saint's celebration. Readings for solemnities and feasts are always proper (specific to the day and obligatory), but even if the day of celebration is a memorial, these specific texts are obligatory.[22] Readings for saints without assigned readings, or for whom additional options could be used, are found in the "Commons." There a great variety of Scripture was compiled for each category of saint: the Blessed Virgin Mary, Martyrs, Pastors, Doctors of the Church, Virgins, and Holy Men and Women, as well as for the Anniversary of the Dedication of a Church. Thus if no

---

19 Adam, 224–228.

20 Jason J. McFarland, "An Overview of Universal Norms on the Liturgical Year and the General Roman Calendar," *The Liturgy Documents, Volume One: Fifth Edition; Essential Documents for Parish Worship* (Chicago: Liturgy Training Publications), 205.

21 Bugnini, 423.

22 Introduction to the Lectionary, 83.

obligatory texts were assigned to a saint, Scripture could be chosen from the appropriate Commons. Celebrations of saints with solemnities and feasts, or (in a few cases) with memorials or optional memorials that have obligatory readings, always take precedence over the assigned weekday readings. The choice of Scripture on the day of a saint's memorial or optional memorial, however, must be weighed next to the weekday readings, and pastors are cautioned not to depart too often from the regular weekly cycle of readings. The saint may still be lifted up in the homily, and intercession may be requested in the Prayer of the Faithful, but the readings for the day would be from the weekday Lectionary. The temporal cycle (Proper of Time), which celebrates the mysteries of salvation, should always take precedence.

Ritual Masses, Masses for Various Needs and Occasions, Votive Masses, and Masses for the Dead

The selections in this part of the Lectionary provide a variety of readings appropriate for the need or circumstance. They offer choices for readings from the Old Testament, Responsorial Psalm, New Testament, the Alleluia verse, and the Gospel. They also provide choices for a First Reading from the New Testament, should these liturgies take place during Easter Time. This part of the Lectionary is divided into four sections: Ritual Masses, Masses for Occasions, Votive Masses and Masses for the Dead.

The selections assigned for Ritual Masses offers choices for Christian Initiation, Holy Orders, Religious Profession, Pastoral Care of the Sick and the Dying, Marriage, and the Dedication or Blessing of a Church or an Altar. The section Masses for Various Needs and Occasions collects Scripture under thirty-one topics, including many under the category "For the Church," and others ranging from "Reconciliation" and "In Time of War" to "Refugees and Exiles," "In Time of Earthquake," "For the Family," and "For the Grace of a Happy Death."

Votive Masses celebrate a devotional theme or mystery and are offered with a special intention in mind. Scripture for nineteen Masses is collected here, some of which, like the Most Holy Trinity and All Saints, may be found in the Sunday volume of the Lectionary as well.

Finally, a generous selection of Scripture for Masses for the Dead provides options for the Commemoration of All the Faithful Departed, for funerals, and for memorial Masses.[23] Such a wide range of choices reflects well the Church's solicitude for the dead and those who mourn them.

---

23 Find one-line summaries of each reading on the website of Rev. Felix Just, SJ: http://catholic-resources.org/Lectionary/2002USL-Masses-Dead.htm.

"The dealings [of the compilers] with the secretariats of the various Protestant confessions show that all profoundly desire a revision of the Lectionary and look with sympathy on this undertaking of the Catholic church."

Annibale Bugnini, The Reform of the Liturgy, 416

CHAPTER 5

The Impact of the Lectionary for the Church and Beyond— an Ecumenical Witness

The new Lectionary was devised to provide the Order of Readings as an organic whole. It represents one of the most important reforms initiated by the Second Vatican Council. There can be no question that it has made a transformative contribution to Catholic worship. In addition, the Lectionary, in large measure, restored the Bible itself to average Catholics. While many have noted ways in which it could be improved, it is impossible to overstate the importance of this Lectionary for Catholic worship and Catholic biblical literacy. Not only has it provided Catholics with greater exposure and stimulated better understanding and appreciation of the Bible, but it has also fostered faith formation and parish Bible study. Another outcome has been its contribution to ecumenism—one of the Council's stated aims: to "promote union among all who believe in Christ."[1]

---

1 SC, 1.

While the Lectionary was being formulated in Rome, other Churches were taking note. The American Anglican, Episcopal, and Lutheran Churches were aware that their lectionaries were similar to that of the Roman Catholic Church, and although modified somewhat since the Reformation, their lectionaries were equally as limited. To compensate for this, Lutherans had developed a list of preaching texts to supplement their lectionary. In Protestant churches from the Reformed tradition (for example, Presbyterians and the United Church of Christ, any with the word "Reformed" in their title, and many others), preachers were tasked with choosing one or more passages from the Bible to be read and for preaching on each Sunday. The leaders of these churches recognized that too many pastors tended to have favorite topics and texts that failed to expand their congregation's exposure to the Bible.

The new Catholic Lectionary was hardly published when all three Presbyterian Churches in the United States adapted the Catholic Lectionary, issued it in *The Worshipbook*,[2] and began to use it in 1970, even before most Catholics were using their new Lectionary. This Presbyterian lectionary was soon approved for voluntary use by The Disciples of Christ. In addition, the Episcopal Church issued its own draft revision of the Catholic Sunday Lectionary and approved it for trial use in 1970. Over the course of the next few years a number of churches devised and adopted a lectionary that was a somewhat revised variant version of the Catholic Lectionary. These various lectionaries springing from the Roman Catholic Lectionary changed some of the First or Second Readings but deliberately retained almost all of the Gospel readings, adding or omitting only a few verses. These common Gospel selections were seen to be an expression of unity (although not uniformity) in the western churches.

In 1974, drawing from the Presbyterian, Catholic, and Episcopal lectionaries, the Consultation on Church Union (COCU—sometimes

---

2   Joint Committee on Worship for the Cumberland Presbyterian Church, Presbyterian Church in the United States, and the United Presbyterian Church in the United States of America, *The Worshipbook: Services and Hymns* (Philadelphia: Westminster Press, 1970).

called Church of Christ Uniting) issued another three-year Sunday lectionary that they hoped all would adopt. However, the Lutherans continued to work on their own lectionary but added the COCU decisions to their deliberations. The Disciples of Christ issued their own lectionary in 1974. American Lutherans and United Methodists issued their own lectionaries in 1976. The Episcopal Church replaced its draft revision with the three-year lectionary in the 1979 Book of Common Prayer.

The Consultation on Common Texts (CCT) began to take an interest in this proliferation of very similar lectionaries in North America. This body, made up of representatives of different churches, was designed to prepare common wording of liturgical texts used by its members. The CCT sponsored a conference in Washington, DC, in March of 1978. Catholic, Episcopal, Lutheran, Presbyterian, Reformed, Methodist, United Church of Christ, Anglican Church of Canada, and the United Church of Canada were represented. In addition, Fr. Gaston Fontaine, the secretary to the Lectionary group of the Consilium attended at the invitation of the CCT. While only Catholics and Anglicans are required by their churches to use a Lectionary, at this meeting the other churches reported that over half their congregations were now using one or another of the new three-year systems. They also noted that interest was growing and that their seminaries were fostering the use of lectionaries. From this meeting it was decided that CCT would undertake the process of harmonizing the various three-year lectionaries.

The Common Lectionary was issued in 1983. Like its predecessors, it retained nearly all the same Gospel selections as its Catholic parent. The second readings were chosen from the existing alternatives in the Catholic or denominational tables, although some readings were lengthened. The major change this Lectionary introduced was to the Old Testament selections for the Sundays following Pentecost to Advent.

From Advent to Pentecost (including Ordinary Time in winter),[3] the Common Lectionary retained the system of corresponding the Old Testament reading to the Gospel or Epistle. But after Pentecost it assigned a system of semicontinuous readings from the Old Testament without any consideration of their relationship to the other readings with which they were collected. In Year A the Old Testament readings from Pentecost up to Christ the King moved through Genesis to Judges. In Year B the first readings focus on the Davidic covenant and Wisdom literature. In Year C one finds semicontinuous selections from the prophets with an emphasis on Jeremiah.

Some churches liked the new schema for the Old Testament; others did not. When the Revised Common Lectionary was issued in 1992 it provided for two alternative systems of first readings. One system assigned Old Testament selections that always corresponded to the Gospel. The alternative provided for the system introduced in the Common Lectionary with some modifications. The Revised Common Lectionary also strongly recommended that one form or another needed to be followed consistently throughout the year and that it would be best to remain in one form for three years before considering changing to the other.

After the Revised Common Lectionary was issued, the use of all of the American variants of the Catholic Lectionary were gradually abandoned in its favor. Today this lectionary is the official lectionary of the Episcopal Church in the United States and it is also frequently used by American Baptist Churches, the Community of Christ, the Disciples of Christ, the Evangelical Lutheran Church in America, the Moravian Church in America, the Lutheran Church—Missouri Synod, the Presbyterian Church USA, the Reformed Church in America, the United Church of Christ, the United Methodist Church, and the Unitarian-Universalist Christian Fellowship. It has also been

---

3   The Common Lectionary retained corresponding readings for all the Sundays after Epiphany until Lent.

adopted by churches in Canada, the United Kingdom, the Philippines, and Australia.[4]

Many churches that adopted the Revised Common Lectionary previously had no liturgical seasons apart from the observance of Christmas Day, Maundy Thursday, Good Friday, and Easter. In ending the year with the observance of the Reign of Christ, these churches were adopting the Catholic observance of Our Lord Jesus Christ, King of the Universe (then known simply as Christ the King), introduced in 1925. One significant blessing of Lectionary use is that in many places in the United States, Catholic priests and clergy of many denominations gather to study their readings, especially the Gospel they generally share, to discern how these readings apply to their local situation. The three-year Catholic Sunday Lectionary has been recognized as "Catholicism's greatest gift to Protestant preaching."[5] Catholics should be aware that their Sunday Lectionary has become an important ecumenical blessing the Church has fostered.

---

4   The Revised Common Lectionary is also used by the Anglican Church of Canada, the United Church of Canada, the Evangelical Lutheran Church in Canada, the Mennonite Church Canada, the Church of England, the Church of Scotland, the Church of Wales, the Methodist Church of Great Britain, the Scottish Episcopal Church, the United Reformed Church of the United Kingdom, the Philippine Independent Church, the Episcopal Church of the Philippines, the United Methodist Church in the Philippines, the Apostolic Catholic Church, the Convention of Philippine Baptist Churches, the United Church of Christ in the Philippines, the Anglican Church of Australia, and the Uniting Church of Australia.

5   James White, *Christian Worship in Transition* (Nashville: Abingdon, 1976), 139.

"Since the use of the mother tongue . . . may be of great advantage to the people, the limits of its use may be extended. This will apply in the first place to the readings."

Constitution on the Sacred Liturgy (Sacrosanctum Concilium), 36.2

CHAPTER 6

Versions of the Bible Used in the English Language Lectionaries

Establishing vernacular Bible translations appropriate for proclamation in the liturgy has turned out to be a delicate matter. After the Order of Readings for Mass was promulgated by Paul VI on May 25, 1969, national or regional bishops' conferences were charged with determining which translations of the Bible to authorize for use in the Lectionary in their area.[1] In 1969, the United States Conference of Catholic Bishops approved the use of the New American Bible (NAB), the Revised Standard Version (RSV), and the Jerusalem Bible for the new Lectionary. Lectionaries using these three translations were

---

1   The decree of May 25, 1969 from the Sacred Congregation for Divine Worship says that the conferences will prepare the vernacular translations of the Scripture texts according to norms laid out in the instruction *Comme le prévoit*, On the Translation of Liturgical Texts for Celebrations with a Congregation, promulgated on January 25, 1969 by Paul VI. The texts may come from already existing translations that conform to this instruction or may be newly translated and must be submitted for approval to the Congregation.

published in the United States in 1970. Other national conferences made their own choices.

In 1991, looking toward publication of a new Lectionary for the 1981 second edition of the Order of Readings, the United States Conference of Catholic Bishops approved the use of the New Revised Standard Version (NRSV) for the Lectionary as an added option for parishes. It also approved the use of a 1991 revision of the NAB Psalter (Book of the Psalms) for the Lectionary and commissioned a reworking of other Scripture in the existing NAB Lectionary.

A major concern at this time was the recognition that many of the traditional Bible translations always used male terms to define all humanity. The issue was so prominent at this time in the English-speaking world that nearly every major version of the Bible went through a revision. Among the Catholic versions, revision of the Jerusalem Bible, called the New Jerusalem Bible, was uneven. Texts that were already revised without consideration for inclusive language were printed as is, whereas texts that were still being worked on incorporated inclusive language. While the second edition of the New Testament in the New American Bible made an effort to use more inclusive language, the text of the 1981 edition of the New American Bible was considered unsatisfactory by many, including the American bishops.

Reflecting an earnest response to the high priority the Council placed upon "full, conscious, and active participation in liturgical celebrations,"[2] the bishops' conferences of Canada and the United States issued documents to address the issue of gender-inclusive language. The Canadian bishops wrote that this concern was "rooted in a theological understanding of the church as a communion, . . . in union with God and with one another through Jesus Christ, in the power of the Holy Spirit"[3] and thus, (quoting the *Dogmatic Constitution of the Church, Lumen Gentium*) "there is in Christ and in the church no

---

2   SC, 14.

3   Bishops' Pastoral Team, Canadian Conference of Catholic Bishops, "To Speak As a Christian Community: Pastoral Message on Inclusive Language" (1989), 6. This document

inequality on the basis of race or nationality, social condition or sex."[4] The bishops from the United States gave a different reason for their attention to inclusivity: "Each and every Christian is called to, and indeed has a right to full and active participation in worship." Participation demands that the assembly "recognize and accept the transcendent power of God's word."[5] And lack of inclusivity was seen to hamper that recognition and acceptance.

Using guidelines that had been approved by the Vatican's Sacred Congregation of Rites, predecessor of the Congregation for Divine Worship and the Discipline of the Sacraments, biblical scholars, working with the International Commission for English in the Liturgy (ICEL), adjusted the Lectionary selections from the NAB to address a growing desire for gender-inclusive language.[6] These

---

may be found in *The Liturgy Documents, Volume Two* (Chicago: Liturgy Training Publications, 1999) 243–247.

4   *Dogmatic Constitution on the Church (Lumen Gentium)*, 32.

5   National Conference of Catholic Bishops, "Criteria for the Evaluation of Inclusive Language Translations of Scriptural Texts Proposed for Liturgical Use," (1990).

6   The official document governing translation at the time was *Comme le prévoit*, On the Translation of Liturgical Texts for Celebrations with a Congregation, previously cited. It was intended to guide the work of translators preparing vernacular translations of ritual books as part of the implementation of the *Constitution on the Sacred Liturgy*. Originally published in *Notitiae*, the journal of the Sacred Congregation of Rites, it can be found in current document collections, such as *The Liturgy Documents, Volume Three* (Chicago: Liturgy Training Publications, 2013), 417–425, with an overview by Paul Turner, 410–415.

Among the English-speaking conferences, parts of *Comme le prévoit* (such as paragraph 20) were interpreted to imply that gender-inclusive language was appropriate in some circumstances. ICEL's advisory committee had adopted a resolution on inclusive language in 1975: "The Advisory Committee of ICEL recognizes the necessity in all future translations and revisions to avoid words which ignore the place of women in the Christian community or which seem to relegate women to a secondary role." (Minutes of the Advisory Board Meeting, August 1975.) In 1980, ICEL issued "Statement: The Problem of Exclusive Language with Regard to Women" in *Eucharistic Prayers* (Washington: ICEL, 1980), 12–13. For further explanation of this issue, see Kathleen Hughes, "Inclusive Language: An Issue Come of Age," *Liturgy 90* (May-June 1993): 8–12.

Guidelines for the use of gender-inclusive language in English translations of ritual books were issued by the Canadian Conference of Catholic Bishops in 1989 ("To Speak As a Christian Community: Pastoral Message on Inclusive Language") and by the United States Conference of Catholic Bishops in 1990 ("Criteria for the Evaluation of Inclusive Language Translations of Scriptural Texts Proposed for Liturgical Use").

adjustments were completed in 1992 and a prototype Lectionary for churches in the United States was sent to Rome for approval.

However, the Congregation for Divine Worship and the Discipline of the Sacraments (CDWDS) no longer favored ICEL's preference for dynamic equivalent translation, a method of translation that tries to convey the sense or meaning of the original text in a natural, readable way.[7] In addition, it did not approve of some forms of gender-inclusive translation. Instead, the Congregation now favored more literal, word-for-word translations—a method called "formal equivalence."[8] For these reasons, the text submitted by the United States Bishops was rejected, and a new process began in Rome, with the participation of some Americans, resulting in a Lectionary translation in harmony with Rome's requirements. Given the Church's new official stance, a majority of the bishops voted to approve the new translation in 1997.[9]

The revised Lectionary was introduced in 1998, and it became the only version of the Bible approved for use in the Lectionary in the dioceses of the United States. Shortly after this, the Gospel Readings from the Lectionary were prepared for the publication of a *Book of the Gospels*. Approved in 2000 for the dioceses of the United States, these texts were published soon after in a variety of beautiful editions. As already described, the *Book of the Gospels* is carried in procession, placed on the altar, and then processed to the ambo for the reading of the Gospel, the high point in the Liturgy of the Word.

The history of Canada's Lectionary has been somewhat different. In 1991 the Canadian Conference of Catholic Bishops approved

---

7   Although the document does not use the term, the approach to translation authorized by *Comme le prévoit* has been compared to dynamic equivalence.

8   Formal equivalence was the approach mandated in the document *Liturgiam authenticam*, promulgated in 2001. It pertained to the translation of both liturgical texts and Scripture, requiring that the New Vulgate translation of the Bible published in 1979 by the Vatican (based on the original fourth-century translation by St. Jerome and used by the Church for centuries) be the point of reference in preparing vernacular translations of the Scriptures for Lectionaries.

9   See a more detailed description of this process in Richard J. Clifford, "The Rocky Road to a New Lectionary," *America* (August 16, 1997): 18–22.

the NRSV for their Lectionary, and following an earlier indication by the Vatican on the acceptability of the NRSV translation, had it published immediately. Approval of the NRSV was withdrawn just two years later, largely because of the "inclusive" translation of specific texts which Christian faith considers to refer to Jesus Christ (such as the use of the term "Son of Man" in the Old Testament), and/or which it would be preferable to translate in a way consistent with the Church's liturgical and catechetical heritage. The Canadian Bishops already had several million dollars invested in their Lectionary and continued to use it. However they also began work on a revision of the NRSV, using principals worked out with the Congregation of Divine Worship and the Discipline of the Sacraments and the Congregation for the Doctrine of the Faith. Following Vatican approval, they issued a new Lectionary for Sundays and Solemnities in 2009. Their second volume of the Lectionary, *Lectionary: Ritual Masses, Masses for Various Needs and Occasions, Votive Masses, Masses for the Dead*, was published in September 2014. A *Book of the Gospels* is expected to be published in September 2015, and the Weekday Lectionary is in preparation, with publication projected for late 2016 or early 2017.

Today Catholics worldwide adhere to the same pattern of readings established by the Lectionary in use since 1970. They also follow the general principles for Lectionary use found in the introduction printed in every volume of the *Lectionary for Mass*. However, the various bishops' conferences from English-speaking countries have chosen to use different versions of the English Bible in their lectionaries. While the United States uses a Lectionary translation based on the NAB and Canada one based on the NRSV, Australia, England and Wales, Scotland, Ireland, India, New Zealand, Pakistan, and South Africa use the Jerusalem Bible of 1966 for their lectionaries.[10] The

---

10   The Jerusalem Bible of 1966 is a translation of the French *Bible de Jerusalem*, while the New Jerusalem Bible issued in 1985 is a translation from the original languages and is a more dynamic equivalent translation.

Revised Standard Version (RSV) is also an authorized option in India, and the Antilles use the second Catholic edition of the RSV.

While approving the second edition of the Lectionary in 1997, the United States Conference of Catholic Bishops also resolved to review the translations introduced in this Lectionary with a view to future changes. Since that Lectionary was issued, a complete revision of the Old Testament was incorporated into the New American Bible in 2011. In another development, the *Revised Grail Psalms*, produced by Conception Abbey, received the approval from the Vatican in 2010 and is now the official Psalter for the United States. In addition, the United States Conference of Catholic Bishops is sponsoring a second revised translation of the New Testament, which will be used with the revised Old Testament translation now incorporated into the New American Bible (revised edition) for a future publication of the Lectionary, and will also be used in all catechetical materials. That translation will become the third edition of the New Testament in the New American Bible.

"This expanded and more suitable arrangement of the Introduction first gives a general statement on the essential bond between the word of God and the liturgical celebration,[1] then deals in greater detail with the word of God in the celebration of Mass, and, finally explains the precise structure of the Order of Readings for Mass."

Introduction to the *Lectionary for Mass*, 1

CHAPTER 7

Insights from the Introduction to the Lectionary—an Essential Document

Significantly updated from the Introduction published in the 1969 edition of the Lectionary, the 1998 Introduction has six chapters divided into three parts that cover the areas described in the quotation above.[2] Below is a list of the headings and subheadings of the Introduction. Even a brief survey of these reveals that this document aims to be both visionary and practical. In the preamble and part 1, the Introduction manages to convey the vision and insight of the

---

1   See SC, 35, 56; Paul VI, Apostolic Exhortation, *Evangelii Nuntiandi* (December 8, 1975), 28, 47; *Acta apostolicae sedis* 68 (1976): 24–25, 36–37; Letter, *Dominicae Cenae* (February 24, 1980), 10, 11, 12; *Acta apostolicae sedis* 72 (1980): 134–146.

2   The Introduction precedes each volume of the Lectionary. It can also be found online by searching for "introduction to the Lectionary."

Council's aspirations for the Word of God in the reformed liturgy, and to describe, in both practical and inspiring ways, the unfolding of the Liturgy of the Word at Mass. Every liturgical minister will benefit from this description, but especially celebrants, deacons, homilists, readers, psalmists, and musicians. The authors have left little to chance as they describe in detail the Liturgy of the Word: its elements (the biblical readings, Responsorial Psalm, acclamation before the Gospel, homily, Profession of Faith, Universal Prayer, and periods of silence) and the ministries (including the roles of celebrant, the faithful, deacon, readers, psalmist, and cantor). These descriptions highlight the general character and tone of the proceedings, the appropriate formation of readers,[3] and the effect that the proclamation of the Word should have on the assembly. It seems clear that when the Liturgy of the Word is celebrated well, in accordance with the principles described here, the faithful will be enabled to experience Christ present in the Word, ponder his Paschal Mystery and the sweep of salvation history, and be able to respond in faith.

Introduction to the Lectionary—Headings and Subheadings

PREAMBLE

Chapter I: General Principles for the Liturgical Celebration of the Word of God

    1. Certain Preliminaries

        a) The Importance of the Word of God in the Liturgical Celebration

        b) Terms Used to Refer to the Word of God

        c) The Significance of the Word of God in the Liturgy

---

3 A resource designed to help readers proclaim each reading effectively is *Workbook for Lectors, Gospel Readers, and Proclaimers of the Word*®, issued annually by Liturgy Training Publications. The readings for Sundays and Holydays are reproduced as the Lectionary presents them, in large print and in sense lines, along with commentaries and proclamation advice so that readers can prepare and practice.

2. Liturgical Celebration of the Word of God
   a) The Proper Character of the Word of God in the Liturgical Celebration
   b) The Word of God in the Economy of Salvation
   c) The Word of God in the Liturgical Participation of the Faithful
3. The Word of God in the Life of the People of the Covenant
   a) The Word of God in the Life of the Church
   b) The Church's Explanation of the Word of God
   c) The Connection between the Word of God Proclaimed and the Working of the Holy Spirit
   d) The Essential Bond between the Word of God and the Mystery of the Eucharist

FIRST PART: THE WORD OF GOD IN THE CELEBRATION OF THE MASS

Chapter II: The Celebration of the Liturgy of the Word at Mass
1. The Elements of the Liturgy of the Word and Their Rites
   a) The Biblical Readings
   b) The Responsorial Psalm
   c) The Acclamation before the Reading of the Gospel
   d) The Homily
   e) Silence
   f) The Profession of Faith
   g) The Universal Prayer or Prayer of the Faithful
2. Aids to the Proper Celebration of the Liturgy of the Word
   a) The Place for the Proclamation of the Word of God
   b) The Books for Proclamation of the Word of God in the Liturgy

Chapter III: Offices and Ministries in the Celebration of the Liturgy of the Word within Mass
1. The Function of the President [Priest Celebrant] at the Liturgy of the Word
2. The Role of the Faithful in the Liturgy of the Word
3. Ministries in the Liturgy of the Word

SECOND PART: THE STRUCTURE OF THE ORDER OF
READINGS FOR MASS

Chapter IV: The General Arrangement of Readings for Mass
  1. The Pastoral Purpose of the Order of Readings for Mass
  2. The Principles of Composition of the Order of
     Readings for Mass
     a) The Choice of Texts
     b) The Arrangement of the Readings for Sundays and
        Festive Days
     c) The Arrangement of the Readings for Weekdays
     d) The Readings for Celebrations of the Saints
     e) Readings for Ritual Masses, Masses for Various Needs and
        Occasions, Votive Masses, and Masses for the Dead
     f) The Main Criteria Applied in Choosing and Arranging
        the Readings
        1) The Reservation of Some Books to Particular
           Liturgical Seasons
        2) The Length of the Texts
        3) Difficult Texts
        4) The Omission of Certain Verses
  3. Principles to Be Followed in the Use of the Order of Readings
     a) The Freedom of Choice Regarding Some Texts
        1) The Two Readings before the Gospel
        2) The Longer and Shorter Forms of Texts
        3) When Two Texts are Provided
        4) The Weekday Readings
        5) The Celebrations of the Saints
        6) Other Parts of the Order of Readings
     b) The Responsorial Psalm and the Acclamation before the
        Gospel Reading

Chapter V: Description of the Order of Readings
  1. Advent
     a) The Sundays
     b) The Weekdays
  2. The Christmas Seasons
     a) The Solemnities, Feasts, and Sundays
     b) The Weekdays

3. Lent
   a) The Sundays
   b) The Weekdays
4. The Sacred Triduum and the Easter Season
   a) The Sacred Easter Triduum
   b) The Sundays
   c) The Weekdays
   d) The Solemnities of the Ascension and of Pentecost
5. Ordinary Time
   a) The Arrangement and Choice of Texts
   b) The Sunday Readings
      1) The Gospel Readings
      2) The Old Testament Readings
      3) The Readings from the Apostles
   c) The Readings of the Solemnities of the Lord
      during Ordinary Time
   d) The Weekday Readings

Chapter VI: Adaptations, Translations, and Format of the Order of Readings

1. Adaptations and Translations
2. The Format of Individual Readings
   a) The Biblical References
   b) The Heading
   c) The "Incipit"
   d) The Final Acclamation

The second part of the Introduction concerning the rationale for the structure of the Order of Readings is fascinating reading for anyone who has a love of Scripture and who has been reflecting on the liturgical readings, noticing recurring passages and themes throughout the year, perhaps pondering questions such as: Why do we hear particular things at particular times? and, Why are some passages included and not others? Here in chapter 4 of the Introduction is a detailed explanation of the principles behind the selection and arrangement of the readings—principles that were summarized earlier in chapter 4 of this book (Designing the Lectionary). Included at this point in the Introduction, for example, is discussion of the principles of harmony and semicontinuous reading. Concerning the length of the readings, we read that most often the compilers aimed for a moderate length and in some cases offered a longer and shorter option of the same reading. Here we also learn that some difficult texts were omitted for pastoral reasons. The chapter then turns to the principles for the *use* of the Lectionary—how a celebrant should make choices when options are provided.

Chapter 5 explains at some length the rationale operating in Sunday readings and weekday readings for each liturgical season and for Ordinary Time. Lastly, chapter 6 describes regulations pertaining to translations and publications, and certain details in the layout of each reading in the Lectionary: the biblical references (citations), the formula for the announcement of the proclaimed reading, the "heading" next to the reading in the Lectionary that signals the main theme of the text, the *incipit*, or introductory phrase added to the reading to provide context, such as "At that time," or "Thus says the Lord," and finally, the closing to the reading: "The word of the Lord," which invites the congregation's acclamation, "Thanks be to God."

The clear, practical explanations throughout this document all flow from the vision behind the Lectionary—of the power of the Word of God in the liturgy, so eloquently expressed in the preamble:

> In the hearing of God's word the Church is built up and grows, and in the signs of the liturgical celebration God's wonderful, past works in the history of salvation are presented anew as mysterious realities. God in turn makes use of the congregation of the faithful that celebrates the Liturgy in order that his word may speed on and be glorified and that his name be exalted among the nations. (7)[4]

---

4   See 2 Thessalonians 3:1.

The proclamation of the Word in the liturgy, provided for in the Lectionary, is activated by the Holy Spirit for the good of each and all:

> The working of the Holy Spirit precedes, accompanies, and brings to completion the whole celebration of the Liturgy. But the Spirit also brings home[5] to each person individually everything that in the proclamation of the word of God is spoken for the good of the whole gathering of the faithful. (9)

We find another aspect of the aims of the compilers of the Lectionary in the beginning of the second part of the Introduction, a section called "The Pastoral Purpose of the Order of Readings for Mass":

> The present Order of Readings for Mass, then, is an arrangement of biblical readings that provides the faithful with a knowledge of the whole of God's word, in a pattern suited to the purpose. Throughout the liturgical year, but above all during the seasons of Easter, Lent, and Advent, the choice and sequence of readings are aimed at giving Christ's faithful an ever-deepening perception of the faith they profess and of the history of salvation. (60)[6]

Unlike the content of a course of study, or a systematic reading of biblical texts, the wisdom of Scripture unfolded in the liturgy flows over us in cycles, year by year, offering ever-deeper encounters with Christ and his mysteries. The Introduction helps us appreciate the majestic vision and intricate design of the Lectionary. Recent years have not produced a better description of the compilers' understanding of their theological purposes and of the Lectionary they devised.

---

5   See John 14:15–17, 25–26, 16:15.

6   See Pope Paul VI, Apostolic Constitution, *Missale Romanum*, in *Missale Romanum ex Decreto Sacrosancti Oecumenici Concilii Vaticani II instauratum auctoritate Pauli VI promulgatum* (Typis Polyglottis Vaticanis, 1975), p. 15, quoted in *Missale Romanum ex Decreto Sacrosancti Oecumenici Concilii Vaticani II instauratum auctoritate Pauli VI promulgatum, Ordo lectionum Missae, editio typica altera* (Typis Polyglottis Vaticanis, 1981), p. XXXI.

"Special care must be taken to ensure that the liturgical
books, particularly the Book of the Gospels and the
Lectionary, which are intended for the proclamation of the
Word of God and hence receive special veneration,
are to be in a liturgical action truly signs and symbols
of higher realities and hence should be truly worthy,
dignified, and beautiful."

General Instruction of the Roman Missal, 349

CHAPTER 8

One Lectionary in Four Volumes—a Tour

To publish the full texts of the readings assigned for every occasion requires several volumes. The Lectionary issued in the United States between 1998 and 2002 has four volumes. One option employed was to issue volume I in three separate ritual books, one for each year of the three-year cycles for Sundays and Solemnities. The single-year format helps the books survive over a longer period of time. In addition to large ritual editions, study editions were published—first a study edition of volume I, incorporating all three years in one paperback, and then a study edition of the remainder of the Lectionary.[1]

---

1   Study editions for the Lectionary have been published by several publishers in the United States, including Liturgy Training Publications (volume I in 1999 and a combined volume II, III, and IV in 2002) and in Canada by the Canadian Conference of Catholic Bishops.

Common Features of the Four Volumes

Every ritual volume of the Lectionary opens with a list of the contents of that volume. Printed next in order are the four decrees that issued the Lectionary, or authorized its publication and use.[2] These decrees are followed by the Introduction to the Lectionary already discussed. This Introduction is reproduced in all four volumes. Each volume provides helpful information in addition to the readings, to be described shortly.

The Lectionary is unified by a system of sequential numbers assigned to each celebration or to a group of choices for one or another of the readings for a specified occasion. The numbering is continuous through all four volumes: in volume I, the First Sunday of Advent in Year A is number 1, and in volume IV, the group of Gospel Readings assigned for Funerals for Children Who Died before Baptism is number 1026. The numbers provide a way to identify each Mass or each grouping of options for a Mass. These numbers are also used in an appendix found at the end of each volume that lists every passage used in the Lectionary in biblical order and identifies the volume(s) and number(s) where each is assigned.

Some key elements in the layout of Individual Lectionary readings were enumerated in the Introduction to the Lectionary discussed in the last chapter. A Lectionary entry for each Mass includes the

---

2   These are: (1) the decree of the Sacred Congregation for Divine Worship that issued the first edition of the Lectionary in 1969; (2) the decree of the Sacred Congregation for the Sacraments and Divine Worship that issued the second typical edition in 1981 (the Vatican uses the word "typical" to designate an authoritative Latin text that serves as the official version and prototype for other languages); (3) the decree of the Congregation for Divine Worship and the Discipline of the Sacraments authorizing the second English edition to be used in the United States of America in 1997 for volume I and in 2001 for volumes II, III, and IV; and finally, (4) the decree of the National Conference of Bishops of the United States of America promulgating the American edition of the 1981 Lectionary in 1998 for volume I and in 2001 for volumes II, III, and IV. The American decree of 1998 indicated that second edition of the Sunday Lectionary would be introduced on the First Sunday of Advent of that year. The decree of 2001 indicated that the weekday Lectionary would be introduced on Ash Wednesday 2002, that the four volumes of the second edition of the *Lectionary for Mass* would become mandatory throughout the United States on Pentecost Sunday, 2002, and that the NAB revision discussed earlier was now the only authorized Lectionary for use in the United States.

SECOND SUNDAY OF LENT

FIRST READING

A reading from the Book of Genesis

GENESIS 22:1–2, 9a, 10–13, 15–18

THE SACRIFICE OF ABRAHAM,
OUR FATHER IN FAITH.

God said to Noah and to his sons with him:
"See, I am now establishing my covenant with you
and your descendants after you
and with every living creature that was with you:
all the birds, and the various tame and wild animals
that were with you and came out of the ark.
I will establish my covenant with you,
that never again shall all bodily creatures be destroyed
by the waters of a flood;
there shall not be another flood to devastate the earth."

God added:
"This is the sign that I am giving for all ages to come,
of the covenant between me and you
and every living creature with you:
I set my bow in the clouds to serve as a sign
of the covenant between me and the earth.
When I bring clouds over the earth,
and the bow appears in the clouds,
I will recall the covenant I have made
between me and you and all living beings,
so that the waters shall never again become a flood
to destroy all mortal beings."

The word of the Lord.

Lectionary #26 Second Sunday of Lent, Year B

Lectionary number; the name of the Sunday, solemnity, feast, or memorial (see the example on page 80); and the date for feasts established by the annual calendar. Each Lectionary text for the Mass is labeled (First Reading, Responsorial Psalm, Second Reading, Alleluia, Gospel). For each reading we find the biblical citation (in some cases two—for a longer form and a shorter form), the "heading" (a sentence or phrase expressing the essential theme of the reading), and then just above the text of the reading, the introductory announcement ("A reading from . . . "). The reading itself appears in large type, arranged in sense lines. Sometimes the reading begins with an *incipit*, an added sentence or phrase that sets the context of the excerpt ("At that time . . . ," "Thus says the Lord . . . ,"). The reading ends with the appropriate closing statement: "The word of the Lord" or "The Gospel of the Lord," which elicits the congregation's response: "Thanks be to God" or "Praise to you Lord Jesus Christ."

Since the organization of a Lectionary may not be intuitive for those unfamiliar with ritual books, the tables of contents are invaluable. In order to convey concisely what each volume has to offer, annotated tables of contents are given below. (Annotations are in italics and parentheses.)[3]

Annotated Tables of Contents of the Four Volumes of Lectionary for Mass

---

Volume I: Sundays and Solemnities

Decrees

Sacred Congregation for Divine Worship, 1st Edition, 1969

Sacred Congregation for the Sacraments and Divine Worship, 2nd Edition, 1981

Congregation for Divine Worship and the Discipline of the Sacraments, 1997

National Conference of Catholic Bishops, United States of America, 1998

---

3   The edition of the Lectionary now in use was published from 1998 to 2001, before the third edition of the *Roman Missal*, with which much terminology changed. Any current terms for times and seasons are given in italics and brackets.

Introduction *(See p. 72 in this book.)*

Tables

Table I: Principal Celebrations of the Liturgical Year, 1999–2025

Table II: Order of the Second Readings for Sundays in Ordinary Time

Abbreviations *(for editions in which books of the Bible are abbreviated)*

Proper of Seasons *[Proper of Time] (containing readings for Sunday Masses arranged by season)*

Season of Advent

Season of Christmas *[Christmas Time]*

Season of Lent

Easter Triduum and Season of Easter *[Sacred Paschal Triduum and Easter Time]*

Ordinary Time *(After all the readings for the Sundays of Ordinary Time come the following sections.)*

Alleluia Verses for Sundays in Ordinary Time

Solemnities of the Lord during Ordinary Time

(The Most Holy Trinity, The Most Holy Body and Blood of Christ, The Most Sacred Heart of Jesus)

Common Texts for Sung Responsorial Psalms

(psalm texts that may be sung for entire seasons in lieu of the assigned Lectionary psalm text)

Chrism Mass

Octave of Easter

Solemnities and Feasts of the Lord and Saints

(If the dates of these feasts or solemnities fall on a Sunday, their readings replace the usual Sunday readings.)

February 2, The Presentation of the Lord

March 19, Saint Joseph, Husband of the Blessed Virgin Mary

March 25, The Annunciation of the Lord

June 24, The Nativity of Saint John the Baptist

June 29, Saints Peter and Paul, Apostles

August 6, The Transfiguration of the Lord

August 15, The Assumption of the Blessed Virgin Mary

September 14, The Exaltation of the Holy Cross

November 1, All Saints

November 2, The Commemoration of All the Faithful Departed

November 9, The Dedication of the Lateran Basilica

December 8, The Immaculate Conception of the
Blessed Virgin Mary

Appendix I: Sequences

*(These are Latin texts of three ancient hymns traditionally sung before the
Gospel on Easter, Pentecost, and the Most Holy Body and Blood of Christ.
The use of the Latin is optional. The English text appears with the other
readings on the appropriate day.)*

Appendix II: Table of Readings

*(This is a table of readings listed in the order of the books of the Bible,
indicating by Lectionary number where they may be found in the Lectionary.
Because volume IV had not yet appeared at the time volume I was
published, passages appearing in volume IV are not indicated in volume I.)*

Appendix III: Table of Responsorial Psalms and Canticles

*(This list, in biblical order and using Lectionary numbers, indicates where
each text can be found in the Lectionary.)*

Volumes II and III

Decrees

Introduction

Tables

Table I: Principal Celebrations of the Liturgical Year

Table II: Order of the First Reading for Weekdeays in Ordinary
Time

Volume II: Proper of Seasons *[Proper of Time]*

Weekday Readings, Year I

Volume III: Proper of Seasons *[Proper of Time]*

Weekday Readings, Year II

*(Gospels are the same in each volume. The First Readings and Responsorial
Psalms are unique to each year. In each volume, readings are arranged
as follows:)*

Season of Advent

Season of Christmas *[Christmas Time]*

Season of Lent

Holy Week

Season of Easter *[Easter Time]*

Ordinary Time

(Alternative Alleluia Verses and Sung Responsorial Psalms):

Alleluia Verses before Ascension

Alleluia Verses after Ascension

Alleluia Verses for Weekdays in Ordinary Time

Common Texts for Sung Responsorial Psalms

Proper of Saints

(Provided in both Volume II and Volume III, the Proper of Saints contains entries for every saint with a memorial, feast, or solemnity in the General Roman Calendar or in the calendar for the United States. The entries provide readings for the saint and/or direct the reader to the Commons for additional options; see below. See also, "Readings for Celebrating the Saints," p. 56.)

January

February

March

April

May

June

July

August

September

October

November

December

Commons

(Additional readings are arranged under the following categories. Each category offers a choice of First Readings from the Old Testament and First Readings from the New Testament during Easter, Responsorial Psalms, Second Readings, Alleluia Verses and Verses before the Gospel, and Gospel Readings.)

The Common of the Anniversary of the Dedication of a Church

The Common of the Blessed Virgin Mary

The Common of Martyrs

The Common of Pastors

The Common of Doctors of the Church

The Common of Virgins

The Common of Holy Men and Women

(For example, January 2 is the Memorial of Sts. Basil the Great and Gregory Nazianzen, early Christian doctors of the Church. The Proper of Saints supplies three options for readings: [1] specific readings printed in the January 2 entry for those saints in the Proper of Saints—Ephesians 4:1–7, 11–13, Psalm 23, and Matthew 21:8–1; [2] the Common of Pastors—Lectionary numbers 719, 721, and 722; and [3] the Common of Doctors of the Church—Lectionary numbers 725, 727, 728, 729, and 730.)

Appendix 1: Sequence: Our Lady of Sorrows *(Latin text of the sequence,* Stabat Mater*)*

Appendix 2: Index of Responsorial Psalms and Canticles

Appendix 3: Index of Readings *(These same appendices appear in both volume II and volume III. Citations for the readings are arranged by books of the Bible, next to which are Lectionary numbers placed in columns indicating in which volume of the Lectionary the readings may be found.)*

Volume IV

Decrees

Introduction

Tables *(repeated from volumes II and III)*

Commons *(repeated from volumes II and III)*

Ritual Masses *(Readings for Masses for certain sacraments and sacramentals—see specifics below.)*

I. For the Conferral of Christian Initiation

    1. Catechumenate and Christian Initiation of Adults

        Entrance into the Order of Catechumens

        Election or Enrollment of Names

        First Scrutiny

        Second Scrutiny

        Third Scrutiny

        Presentation of the Creed

        Presentation of the Lord's Prayer

Baptism during the Easter Vigil

Christian Initiation apart from the Easter Vigil

2. Conferral of Infant Baptism

3. Reception of Baptized Christians into the Full Communion of the Catholic Church

4. Confirmation

5. First Communion for Children

II. For the Conferral of Holy Orders

III. For the Admission to Candidacy for the Diaconate and the Priesthood

IV. For the Conferral of Ministries

1. Institution of Readers

2. Institution of Acolytes

V. For the Pastoral Care of the Sick and the Dying

1. Anointing of the Sick

2. Viaticum

VI. For the Conferral of the Sacrament of Marriage

VII. For the Blessing of Abbots and Abbesses

VIII. For the Consecration of Virgins and Religious Profession

IX. For the Dedication or Blessing of a Church or an Altar

1. Dedication of a Church

2. Dedication of an Altar

3. Blessing of a Chalice and Paten

Masses for Various Needs and Occasions

I. For the Holy Church

(Few people realize that the Church has provided for liturgical observances that would fit almost any situation. In this section are listed thirty-one occasions with a variety of passages for each reading.)

1. For the Church

2. For the Pope or a Bishop, especially on their anniversaries

3. For the Election of a Pope or Bishop

4. For a Council or Synod or a Spiritual or Pastoral Meeting

5. For Priests

6. For Ministers of the Church

7. For Religious

8. For Vocations to Holy Orders or Religious Life
9. For the Laity
10. For the Unity of Christians
11. For the Evangelization of Peoples
12. For Persecuted Christians.

II. For Public Needs

13. For the Country or a City or For Those Who Serve in Public Office or For the Congress or For the President or For the Progress of Peoples
14. For Peace and Justice
15. For Reconciliation
16. In Time of War of Civil Disturbance

III. In Various Public Circumstances

17. For the Beginning of the Civil Year
18. For the Blessing of Human Labor
19. For Productive Land
20. After the Harvest
21. In Time of Famine or For those Who Suffer from Famine
22. For Refugees and Exiles
23. For Those Held Captive
24. For the Sick
25. In Time of Earthquake or For Rain or For Good Weather or To Avert Storms or for Any Need
26. In Thanksgiving to God

IV For Various Needs

27. For the Remission of Sins
28. For the Promotion of Charity or To Foster Harmony or For Family and Friends
29. For the Family
30. For Our Oppressors
31. For the Grace of a Happy Death

Votive Masses

(Votive Masses are celebrated to foster particular Catholic devotions.)

The Most Holy Trinity

The Mystery of the Holy Cross

The Most Holy Eucharist

Jesus Christ, the Eternal High Priest

The Most Holy Name of Jesus

The Most Precious Blood of Our Lord Jesus Christ

The Most Sacred Heart of Jesus

The Holy Spirit

The Blessed Virgin Mary

    I. The Blessed Virgin Mary, Mother of the Church

    II. The Most Holy Name of Mary

The Holy Angels

Saint Joseph

All the Holy Apostles

Saints Peter and Paul, Apostles

Saint Peter, Apostle

Saint Paul, Apostle

One Holy Apostle

All the Saints

Masses for the Dead

(A great treasury of readings for all the liturgies associated with funerals is provided here and may also be found in the Order of Christian Funerals. These selections, grouped in sections for adults and children, may also be used for the Commemoration of All the Faithful Departed or any memorials or anniversaries.)

    Masses for the Dead

    Funerals for Baptized Children

    Funerals for Children Who Died before Baptism

Appendices *(repeated from volumes II and III)*

The Lectionary as a Liturgical Object

All ritual books (of which there are many besides the Lectionary and *Book of the Gospels*, including the *Roman Missal*) are designed not only to contain content, but to function as liturgical objects. The celebration of Mass, as a meeting between Christ and the People of God,

The *Book of the Gospels* carried in the entrance procession.

calls for dignity, reverence, and joy. Because the Sacred Scriptures are the Word of God, inspired by the Holy Spirit, the physical book from which the Scriptures are proclaimed should be dignified and reverently treated. While the biblical readings are printed in a variety of forms, such as short-term paper missals, hymnbooks, personal missals, and so forth, a ritual book is the *only* appropriate one from which to proclaim the readings during Mass.

The first two readings must come from the Lectionary, placed open on the ambo before Mass begins. If the parish owns a *Book of the Gospels*, the elegant book containing the Gospel Readings from the Lectionary, that book is the only one to be carried in procession. Parishes that do not own a *Book of the Gospels* should not substitute the Lectionary in opening processions, nor should the Lectionary be honored with incense. The Lectionary, like the *Roman Missal*, contains important texts for the Mass used by a single minister. Neither of these books is elevated and displayed to the assembly. They should be dignified, handsome, sturdy, and handled respectfully, but they keep a low profile in contrast to the *Book of the Gospels*.

Nevertheless both the Lectionary and the *Book of the Gospels* contain God's Word and are sacred— symbolic as well as practical. In some cultures, when a sacred book is carried into the liturgy, people stretch out their hands to touch it. The *Book of the Gospels*, especially, is one of the ways Christ is present to us. Imagine Simon Peter speaking to Jesus: "Master . . . you have the words of eternal life" (John 6:68). The beauty of a *Book of the Gospels* and the rituals with which we surround it can awaken the community's affection and reverence for the Word of God. Many editions of the *Book of the Gospels* have elaborate, eye-catching covers, designed to be seen from afar when the book is held up in a procession. Often the interior is filled with art, and at some parishes, a special stand allows illustrated pages of the book to be displayed in the church outside of the liturgy.[4]

The beauty of a *Book of the Gospels* and the rituals with which we surround it can awaken the community's affection and reverence for the Word of God.

As a practical matter, there may be occasions when readings are chosen from a variety of places in the Lectionary. While the Lectionary may be marked with ribbons and a particular reading on a page flagged by a sticky note that can be removed without harming the book, some readers would find it confusing to turn to readings marked in different parts of the book. In these instances, the readings could be reproduced in large print, using the sense lines of the original layout, and collected in order in a handsome hardcover liturgical binder, such as those available commercially in liturgical colors.

---

4   Two editions of the *Book of the Gospels* produced in the United States include original art: Liturgy Training Publications (Chicago) uses art in the Ethiopian Christian style by Laura James and Liturgical Press (Collegeville, MN) uses art from the remarkable hand-illuminated Bible it commissioned by Donald Jackson, the *Saint John's Bible*.

" . . . to adapt more suitably to the needs of our own times
those institutions that are subject to change."

Constitution on the Sacred Liturgy (Sacrosanctum Concilium), 1

CHAPTER 9

Problems and Omissions in the Lectionary

The Lectionary is a vital liturgical resource of inestimable significance for Catholic worship and a marvelous example of ecumenical witness. For more than forty-five years, the Catholic faithful have been learning the skill of attentive listening with a range of Scripture texts that were vastly expanded from days before the Council and positioned throughout the liturgical year. Sunday by Sunday, as the Word of God joins with the sounds and actions of the liturgy and human time blends with sacred time, the assembly becomes more saturated in the mysteries of the faith.

Despite the enormous increase in Scripture incorporated into Catholic liturgy by the Lectionary, some Catholics, especially Scripture scholars, came to recognize that many memorable stories do not appear in the Sunday Lectionary and that many women who are mentioned in the Bible as participants in the unfolding of salvation history are not included among the selections. Others expressed concerns about some selections pertaining to Jews and Judaism. The Pontifical Biblical Commission, in its document *The Interpretation of the Bible in the Church* (presented to Pope John Paul II in March of 1993), recognized that while the Council Fathers called for a Sunday Lectionary to be "more ample, more varied and more suitable,"[1] "in its present state," the Commission wrote, "it only partially fulfills this goal."[2]

The Commission's words express in a general way concerns circulating at the time that identified as significant issues the absence of many stories, the overly brief selections of many texts, and the prominence of typology as an underlying principle for relating Old Testament and Gospel passages.

While the Holy Spirit continues to inspire and refresh the Church through the insights of its leaders and scholars, the monumental task of revising the Lectionary will not be undertaken in the near future. At the present time it is important to identify issues that need amelioration.

Short Readings

One reason that some readings in the Lectionary are short may stem from a phase in its development. During the process of devising the Lectionary, some European churches were asked to try out some of the collections of readings. Considering that the people were used to short readings in Latin (with, perhaps, a vernacular translation before the homily), and that in this trial sample four Scripture passages were suddenly introduced without much, if any, preparatory explanation, it is not surprising that the parishes found the readings too long. As a result of that early feedback, many selections —especially those from the Old Testament—were abbreviated.

Today worshiping assemblies often complain that many readings are far too short. Indeed homilists must frequently make a special effort to fill in the rest of the story so that the passage is

---

1   SC, 35.

2   Pontifical Biblical Commission, "The Interpretation of the Bible in the Church," 224, in *The Bible Documents: A Parish Resource* (Chicago: Liturgy Training Publications, 2001).

understandable. This problem is especially acute with respect to the Old Testament selections.[3]

Typology

As noted earlier, (p. 50), the Lectionary follows the general practice of typology: matching an Old Testament passage with that of a Gospel. In some cases the passages correspond because of a similar person, symbol, or situation. In other instances an event in the Old Testament passage foreshadows that of Christ in the Gospel selection. While early Christian writers favored this approach, the Pontifical Biblical Commission noted that typology "is not the only interpretation possible."[4] In 2001, the Pontifical Biblical Commission set this observation in a broader context in *The Jewish People and Their Sacred Scripture in the Christian Bible*, a document that explained the difference between Christian readings of Old Testament passages and those of ancient Israel, as well as contemporary Jews, noting that Christians benefit from understanding how Israel heard God speaking to them in their own contexts through their sacred texts.[5] On this issue, many Scripture scholars have observed that a continuous reading of Old Testament books, as employed in the Revised Common Lectionary (described above) offers a more comprehensive appreciation of the Old Testament than that of the present Roman Catholic Sunday Lectionary.

Jews and Judaism

Concerns about the role of Old Testament Scripture in the Lectionary pertain not only to the interpretation of Scripture, but they also have

---

3 At the Washington, DC, meeting that led to the development of the Common Lectionary, a prominent critique of the Catholic Lectionary, as well as its variants, was the shortness of the Old Testament readings and the absence of many important stories from the Old Testament.

4 Pontifical Biblical Commission, "The Interpretation of the Bible in the Church," 224.

5 Pontifical Biblical Commission, *The Jewish People and Their Sacred Scripture in the Christian Bible* (2001), section A 2.

implications for the lessons we draw from Scripture about our relationship with the Jewish people. In 1965, the Second Vatican Council issued its revolutionary document *Nostra Aetate* ("In our time . . . ")—in English, *Declaration on the Relation of the Church to the Non-Christian Religions*.[6] This Council document corrected several erroneous but widespread Christian beliefs and attitudes held throughout the centuries.

Among its teachings, four are especially important. First, far from considering herself opposed to and estranged from Judaism, the Church appreciates Christianity's roots in Judaism, from which it still draws nourishment. Jesus and the Apostles were Jews and reverenced the Scriptures of Israel that became the Christian Old Testament. Second, what Christians identify as the "Old Testament" records God's first revelation, and that revelation was to Israel. Third, and most significantly, most Jews at the time of Jesus and throughout subsequent history are neither responsible nor culpable for the death of Jesus Christ, a belief that has resulted in much persecution and anti-Judaism. Christ freely chose his sacrifice for the sake of our salvation. Finally, the Church does not believe that God's love for and call to the Jews as his "Chosen People" has changed. It remains in force. The Church does not supersede Israel.

Since then, several other Church documents have followed, notably, two issued by the Vatican, *Guidelines and Suggestions for Implementing the Conciliar Declaration "Nostra Aetate" (n. 4)* and *Notes on the Correct Way to Present the Jews and Judaism in Preaching and Catechesis in the Roman Catholic Church*. In addition, another was issued by the United Stated Conference of Catholic Bishops, *God's Mercy Endures Forever, Guidelines on the Presentation of Jews and Judaism in Catholic Preaching*.[7] All three of these subsequent documents sought

---

6 *Nostra Aetate*, 4.

7 Vatican Commission for Religious Relations with the Jews, *Guidelines and Suggestions for Implementing the Conciliar Declaration "Nostra Aetate" (n. 4)* (1974), and by the same commission, *Notes on the Correct Way to Present the Jews and Judaism in Preaching and Catechesis in the Roman Catholic Church* (1985); Bishops' Committee on the Liturgy, National Conference

to make the Church's position expressed in *Nostra Aetate* better known to Catholics. They especially aimed to encourage homilists and catechists to counter misimpressions with sound teaching on the occasions when it can be most formative, in homilies and in catechesis.

Some may ask, why are there misimpressions? The Church realized that some Scriptures heard in the liturgy, if they are not explained and put in context, can convey the very impressions that *Nostra Aetate* was at pains to correct.[8] Biblical scholars had long recognized that the New Testament reflects the painful events unfolding during the second half of the first century, the time when the letters of Paul and the Gospel accounts were written. Jewish Christians, who disagreed with their fellow Jews on the most authentic ways to be faithful to their ancient traditions, were in the process of being expelled or separating from the synagogues and from their roots; they were angry with those who rejected the Gospel. The bitter feelings of later decades were projected back into Jesus' story, at times portraying the conflict between Jesus and his rivals as a condemnation of most of his fellow Jews. In addition, these early Christians lived in the Roman Empire and experienced persecution by Rome before most of the New Testament was written. In recounting Jesus' death, it appears that Roman responsibility was somewhat diminished, while Jewish complicity and culpability expanded. In light of this, the Committee on Divine Worship of the United States Conference of Catholic Bishops urges preachers to "confront misinterpretations of

The Church realized that some Scriptures heard in the liturgy, if they are not explained and put in context, can convey the very impressions that *Nostra Aetate* was at pains to correct.

---

of Catholic Bishops, *God's Mercy Endures Forever, Guidelines on the Presentation of Jews and Judaism in Catholic Preaching* (September, 1988).

8   The compilers of the Lectionary were working even before *Nostre Aetate* was issued. The implications of a document mandating such a revolutionary change in traditional thinking likely was not fully appreciated at the time.

the meaning of the lectionary readings, which have been too familiar in the past" and to that end points out where problems arise in the readings throughout the liturgical year.[9]

The most egregious example of a passage that has caused devastating persecution of Jews on the part of Christians is that of Matthew 27:25. At many moments in the history of Christianity, Christians took literally the passage, "His blood be upon us and upon our children," and were convinced that Jews of all generations were guilty for the death of Jesus. We hear this line proclaimed on Palm Sunday in Year A. But while the full significance of this line is likely to be missed in the very long Passion narrative of Palm Sunday, on Easter Sunday and during Easter, in the First Reading from the Acts of the Apostles, we hear speeches by Peter addressed to Jews accusing them of killing Jesus. The Vatican document *Guidelines and Suggestions* makes specific recommendations about this problem to Scripture translators preparing texts for liturgical proclamation:

> Obviously, one cannot alter the text of the Bible. The point is that, with a version destined for liturgical use, there should be an overriding preoccupation to bring out explicitly the meaning of a text,[1] while taking scriptural studies into account.
>
> [And in footnote 1:] Thus the formula "the Jews," in St. John, sometimes according to the context means "the leaders of the Jews," or "the adversaries of Jesus," terms which express better the thought of the evangelist and avoid appearing to arraign the Jewish people as such.[10]

Like the Vatican Committee on Religious Relations with the Jews, the Bishops' Committee on the Liturgy also finds that regularly pairing Old Testament readings with Gospel Readings so that the older text is seen to prefigure Christ can seem to imply that the Old Testament has no meaning except as a prophecy of Christ. In fact many Catholic Scripture scholars find it vital for Christians to read

---

9   *God's Mercy Endures Forever*, 9, 11–26, 31–32.

10 *Guidelines and Suggestions*, section 2.

the Old Testament both for its meaning to ancient Jewish readers and for the light it sheds on the Gospel.[11]

In discussions of this issue, some authorities maintain that passages prone to misunderstanding should be retained and explained in the homily. Many others point out that good preaching and teaching cannot be assumed and, following the Lectionary's own guidelines (that passages with pastoral difficulties may be omitted), urge eliminating those lines with the potential to foster anti-Judaism.[12] The United States Conference of Catholic Bishops has made available on its website the 1985 revision of its document *Guidelines for Catholic-Jewish Relations*, which includes specific recommendations about homilies and the presentation of the Crucifixion story during Holy Week. Other pastoral resources also exist.[13]

The Witness of Biblical Women

The Biblical Movement that developed in the United States in the 1950s and especially the introduction of the new Lectionary in 1970 stimulated a new interest in biblical texts. Significant numbers of Catholic women were inspired to take up advanced studies of the Bible and other theological disciplines. At the same time, a heightened awareness about injustices pertaining to race, class, and gender arose in North America and Europe, and these concerns were in the minds of many women pursuing advanced studies.

Female Scripture scholars came to recognize that biblical translations using male terms to speak of all humanity marginalized women's experience in the sacred texts. The insight won support from many biblical experts and prompted new inclusive-language

---

11 *God's Mercy Endures Forever*, 14–15.

12 See paragraph 77 of the Introduction to the *Lectionary for Mass*.

13 See, under "Recommended Programs," paragraph 4 and 10b at http://www.usccb.org/prayer-and-worship/liturgical-year/lent/guidelines-for-catholic-jewish-relations.cfm. Another important resource is John T. Pawlikowski's book, *When Catholics Speak about Jews: Notes for Homilists and Catechists* (Chicago: Liturgy Training Publications, 1987). Although out of print, it can often be found through online booksellers.

editions of the Bible, yet it was soon recognized that gender-inclusive language alone did not rectify the issue. As women in the academy began to focus on the analysis of specific stories and images of women in the Bible, more attentive Catholics (biblical scholars and liturgists—both women and men, liturgists, women religious, and even some men and women in the pews) observed that the Lectionary failed to include many stories of the women who have important roles in the biblical narrative. Women are absent from many of the stories told in the Lectionary, hidden in very long selections, or dropped from suggested shorter readings. For example, First Readings from the Old Testament include only eight selections that introduce only four women as participants in the stories of Israel. While the Gospel selections include the stories of the male followers of Jesus from more than one Gospel, only the stories of the women's discovery of Jesus' empty tomb are included from all three synoptic Gospels in the Lectionary. In addition, the only story of Jesus' healing that is not included in the Lectionary is that of the bent woman from Luke (13:10–17), the woman Jesus identified as a "daughter of Abraham," who likely suffered from osteoporosis.[14] The story of the woman who anoints Jesus' head in a symbolic declaration of Jesus as the Son of God, the woman of whom Jesus says "wherever the gospel is proclaimed to the whole world, what she has done will be told in memory of her," (Mark 14:9) is hidden in the very long Passion narrative on Palm Sunday in Year B. Her story is omitted from Matthew's account in Year A and absent from the approved shorter Gospel reading for Year B.

Some of the early reports of this concern were comprehensive and clearly reflected a feminist exasperation;[15] others were more

---

14 The reading appears in the Lectionary for Weekdays, #479, Monday of the Thirtieth Week in Ordinary Time.

15 For example, Regina A. Boisclair, "Amnesia in the Catholic Sunday Lectionary," ed. Mary Ann Hinsdale and Phyllis H. Kaminiski, *Women and Theology: The Annual Publication of the College Theology Society* 40 (Orbis, 1995): 109–135.

irenic.[16] The problem was not limited to the Roman Catholic Sunday Lectionary; it was also clearly identified in the Common Lectionary.[17] While this issue has yet to be addressed in the Catholic Lectionary, the committee charged with the revision of the Common Lectionary (discussed on p. 62) took these concerns into account and introduced more women's stories in the Revised Common Lectionary, used today in many Protestant and Anglican churches.

The poor representation of women and the lack of female biblical images in the Catholic Lectionary have stimulated a number of attempts to fill in the gaps with resources intended for personal reading and prayer and for group study outside the liturgy.[18] They have also motivated scholarly research in Scripture and in pastoral liturgy.

---

16 Eileen Schuller, "Women in the Lectionary," *National Bulletin on Liturgy* 27, no. 137 (1994): 108–14.

17 Marjorie Procter Smith, *In Her Own Rite: Constructing Feminist Liturgical Tradition* (Nashville: Abingdon Press, 1990).

18 One example is J. Frank Henderson, *Remembering the Women: Women's Stories from Scripture for Sundays and Festivals* (Chicago: Liturgy Training Publications, 1999). This book assigns one reading about women, Wisdom, or another feminine image for each Sunday and Solemnity of the year in each year of the three-year cycle. When relevant passages appear in the Roman Catholic Lectionary or Revised Common Lectionary, those are used. In other cases, alternative readings from either Old or New Testament are supplied.

All these things have been arranged in this way so as to
arouse more and more among Christ's faithful that hunger
for the Word of God[1] . . . [so] that, meditating more deeply
on Sacred Scripture, they will be nourished more abundantly
each day by the words of the Lord.

Paul VI, *Apostolic Constitution, Promulgation of the "Missale Romanum"*
Renewed by Decree of the Second Ecumenical Council of the Vatican

CHAPTER 10

Experiencing the Lectionary

Reading the Bible to Hear the Lectionary

Many resources have been developed to help Catholics read and ponder the Lectionary readings outside of the liturgy, and at many parishes groups meet to discuss the readings. Whether considering each
reading separately or teasing out the insights sparked by their relationships to each other, the faithful have been finding a great feast in
the Lectionary.

Even as the Lectionary nourishes us with the readings, it also
invites us to expand our menu to the Bible itself. In fact, as the
Scripture scholar and Lectionary expert Normand Bonneau writes,

the Sunday Eucharist cannot pretend to be the first and foremost
occasion for the faithful to be exposed to and become familiar with the
scriptures. The Lectionary presupposes an adequate acquaintance with

---

1   See Amos 8:11.

the Bible. It serves an anamnetic purpose, to recall and evoke the key moments and reflections of the history of salvation centered in the paschal mystery.[2]

The Pontifical Biblical Commission, in *The Interpretation of the Bible in the Church*, notes how much Scripture now permeates the liturgy and expresses concern about the people's capacity to absorb "the language of the Bible and the symbolism it contains." It comments, "How necessary it is, therefore, that participation in the liturgy be prepared for and accompanied by the practice of reading Scripture."[3] Happily, since the Lectionary's introduction in 1970, interest has grown substantially in Catholic Bible study groups. That "warm and living love for Scripture" that the Council fathers so wished to promote, is taking root.[4]

The "backstory" of the Bible's great characters, the historical and geographical contexts of events, the earlier and subsequent plot twists of the great stories of the Bible—all of these are so easily missed when the congregation hears only a short episode from a story. The listening congregation will be better engaged and understand more if they already know the plots, characters, and contexts of the readings they hear proclaimed at Mass. Although the Lectionary certainly does feed people who know only the Scripture they encounter in the liturgy, the great mosaic presented by the Lectionary, piece by piece, will come to life more vividly if the faithful are reading Scripture regularly outside of Mass.

Attentive Listening as a Spiritual Skill

As is well known, the people's "full, conscious, and active participation in liturgical celebrations" was "the aim to be considered before all else" by the Council fathers.[5] The most efficacious form of

---

2   Bonneau, 49.

3   *Interpretation of the Bible in the Church*, 225.

4   SC, 24.

5   Ibid., 14.

participation during the proclamation of Scripture in the Liturgy of the Word is attentive listening: "The participation of the faithful in the Liturgy increases to the degree that, as they listen to the word of God proclaimed in the Liturgy, they strive harder to commit themselves to the Word of God incarnate in Christ."[6]

Over and over, documents referring to the role of Scripture in the reformed liturgy speak of listening. Often this occurs as a direct instruction: "The readings from the Word of God are to be listened to reverently by everyone, for they are an element of the greatest importance in the Liturgy,"[7] or "The faithful listen to God's word and meditate on it."[8] Sometimes the documents refer to listening indirectly. Explaining the purpose of the Introductory Rites, the *General Instruction of the Roman Missal* (GIRM) says that through those rites, the faithful "dispose themselves properly to listen to the Word of God"[9]—they begin to leave behind their preoccupations and prepare to focus on the liturgy. In discussing the homily, the GIRM refers to the faithful as "the listeners."[10] Being "a listener" is the task and identity of every faithful participant, even the celebrant ("he too is a listener to the word of God proclaimed by others"), yet he must also "help the people listen more attentively" through his introductory comments and the homily.[11] Much in the liturgy is arranged to facilitate the work of listening. Describing in detail the appropriate physical

"the faithful . . . are to listen to the word of God with an inward and outward reverence that will bring them to continuous growth in the spiritual life and draw them more deeply into the mystery which is celebrated."
Introduction to the *Lectionary for Mass*, 45

---

6   Introduction to the *Lectionary for Mass*, 6.

7   GIRM, 29.

8   Introduction, 8.

9   GIRM, 46.

10 Ibid., 65.

11 Introduction, 38.

location for the proclamation of the readings, the Introduction to the Lectionary stipulates that "the place for the readings must also truly help the people's listening and attention during the liturgy of the word."[12] In a wonderful echo of Abraham and Moses receiving God's words of covenant in ancient times, the Introduction to the Lectionary says "the congregation of Christ's faithful even today receives from God the word of his covenant through the faith that comes by hearing."[13] "The faith that comes by hearing" is an evocative phrase for reflection.

Especially interesting is the way the Introduction characterizes listening, for example, in this eloquent description: "When God communicates his word, he expects a response, one that is, of listening and adoring 'in Spirit and in truth' (John 4:23)." Listening that also involves adoring "in Spirit and in truth" bears fruit, the Introduction assures us, for "the Holy Spirit makes that response effective, so that what is heard in the celebration of the Liturgy may be carried out in a way of life: 'Be doers of the word and not hearers only' (James 1:22)."[14] Later in the Introduction we read that "the faithful . . . are to listen to the word of God with an inward and outward reverence that will bring them to continuous growth in the spiritual life and draw them more deeply into the mystery which is celebrated."[15] This characterization of listening as a spiritual practice taps into a long tradition, especially strong in monasticism. The prologue to St. Benedict's Rule begins: "Listen carefully, my son [daughter], to the master's instructions, and attend to them with the ear of your heart."[16] Listening to the proclamation of the Word does indeed engage hearts as well as minds, require detachment from worldly cares, and

---

12 Ibid., 32.

13 Ibid., 45.

14 Ibid., 6.

15 Ibid., 45.

16 Timothy Fry, ed., *RB1980: The Rule of St. Benedict in Latin and English with Notes* (Collegeville, Minnesota: The Liturgical Press, 1981).

encourage focus on the presence of Christ in our midst. It is a skill to be practiced and cultivated.

The Lectionary: A Lens for Experiencing the Mystery of the Mass

As the heart of the Catholic faith, the Mass gathers us, a holy people, in sacred space at an appointed time and engages our minds, hearts, and bodies with holy things so that we become aware of the presence of the Father, Son, and Holy Spirit and the accompaniment of all the saints. The Mass calls us into an act of deep remembrance of everything the Sacred Scriptures tell us as we share the Body and Blood of Christ. In doing this, all time is unified in one today and all believers in one community, offering praise to the Father through the Son. Through this we are changed.

Just as the liturgical year furnishes the frame for the Lectionary, the Lectionary provides the lens for experiencing the mystery of the Mass. The biblical readings are not merely read; they are proclaimed, and that very proclamation makes present the God who has called us into an encounter. Our response in faith is possible because of God's initiative and promise to be with us always.[17] Arrayed in the framework of the liturgical year, the readings offer participants particular episodes in the story of salvation, particular aspects of the Paschal Mystery through which to experience the Mass. On any given day, the episode or aspect proclaimed in the readings and explained in the homily during the Liturgy of the Word mingles with the joys and sorrows we have brought with us and focuses all the ritual words and actions in the Liturgy of the Eucharist. Individual predispositions may determine how one attends and participates; those who gather to worship with full, active participation want to hear the readings, take to heart the counsels of Scripture, and hear the story of Jesus and his call to follow.

---

17 Aiden Kavanaugh, *On Liturgical Theology* (New York: Pueblo, 1984), 91–2.

"Lex supplicandi legem statuat credendi": "Let the law of prayer determine the law of faith," wrote Prosper of Aquitaine in the early fifth century.[18] Indeed, after the Resurrection, the Apostles had to live in a new reality. They did so in gathering to pray, to read the Scriptures, to sing, and to meet the Risen Christ by doing what he had asked them to do in memory of him. In these first Eucharistic liturgies, the faith of the Church was forged. Ever since, the faith of the Church is constantly affirmed and renewed in these liturgies. The Lectionary provides selections of Scripture arranged and ordered in time—a program shaped by the faith of the Church, at the center of which is Jesus Christ and his Paschal Mystery.[19] That faith is renewed and affirmed when the readings are proclaimed. Looking through the lens of the Lectionary, we are nourished and changed by the mystery of the Mass.

---

18 *Capitula Coelestini*, 8: PL 51, 210.

19 Thomas L. Leclerc, "The Sunday Lectionary as Biblical Interpreter," *Liturgical Ministry* 13 (Fall, 2004): 179: "It is the faith of the Church that shapes the Lectionary."

GLOSSARY

Canon A collection of sacred writings accepted as authentic.

Continuous and Semicontinuous Reading Continuous reading in the Lectionary includes the entire biblical text, one day's reading picking up where the previous one has left off. Semicontinuous reading skips over parts of the biblical text so that one day's reading does not pick up exactly where the previous one left off.

Ember days Before the reform of the liturgical year after the Second Vatican Council, ember days were the four sets of Wednesday, Friday, and Saturday designated as days of prayer, fasting, and penitence and occurring in spring (after the First Sunday of Lent), summer (after Pentecost Sunday), autumn (after the Invention of the True Cross—now called the Exaltation of the Holy Cross), and winter (after the Feast of St. Lucy).

Epistle Literally, a letter—either written by a known teacher from the time of the Apostles or by an unknown follower at a later date.

Explicit A Latin word designating the last word or words of a text.

Feast In the liturgical year, a day of celebration of the second rank (solemnities being first and memorials being third and optional memorials being fourth).

Incipit A Latin word designating the first word or words of a text. In the context of the Liturgy of the Word, the *incipit* is often an added phrase that supplies the context of the reading that would otherwise be lost: "At that time," "Brothers and Sisters," "Beloved," or "Thus says the Lord."

Memorial In the liturgical year, a day of celebration of the third rank (solemnities and feasts being first and second, optional memorials being fourth).

Ordinary Time Counted time, an ordered sequence of time in the liturgical year distinct from the liturgical seasons of Advent, Christmas Time, Lent, the Sacred Paschal Triduum, and Easter Time. Ordinary Time begins on the Monday following the Sunday occurring after January 6 and runs through the Tuesday before Ash Wednesday. It resumes on the Monday following Pentecost Sunday and stretches to the Solemnity of Our Lord Jesus Christ, King of the Universe, the last Sunday of the year.

Pericope The shortest section of a text that tells a complete story; derived from a Greek word meaning the act of cutting.

Proper of Saints or Sanctoral Cycle The arrangement or system of days in the liturgical year on which the saints are celebrated. The sanctoral cycle is interwoven with the temporal cycle in the liturgical year.

Proper of Time or Temporal Cycle The arrangement or system of days and seasons in the liturgical year that celebrate events or concepts in the life of Jesus Christ or salvation history.

Solemnity In the liturgical year, a day of celebration of the first rank.

Synoptic Gospels Matthew, Mark, and Luke—those Gospel accounts that cover approximately the same content. John, by contrast, has a different arrangement and content.

Typology An approach to Scripture interpretation that sees in the Old Testament a "type" (aspect of Christ or of a Christian event or doctrine) that is described in the New Testament. The Old Testament type prefigures the New.

FURTHER READING

Church Documents

Second Vatican Council. *Constitution on the Sacred Liturgy* (*Sacrosanctum Concilium*). 1963. In *The Liturgy Documents, Volume One: Fifth Edition; Essential Documents for Parish Worship*. Chicago: Liturgy Training Publications, 2012. (Also available on the Vatican website.)

Second Vatican Council. *Dogmatic Constitution on Divine Revelation* (*Dei Verbum*). 1965. In *The Bible Documents*. Chicago: Liturgy Training Publications, 2001. (Also available on the Vatican website.)

Introduction to the *Lectionary for Mass*. 1998. In *The Liturgy Documents, Volume One: Fifth Edition; Essential Documents for Parish Worship*. Chicago: Liturgy Training Publications, 2012. (Also available in any volume of the *Lectionary for Mass*, in *The Bible Documents*, cited above, and on the Vatican website.)

General Instruction of the Roman Missal, Including Adaptations for the Dioceses of the United States of America. 2011. In *The Liturgy Documents, Volume One: Fifth Edition; Essential Documents for Parish Worship*. Chicago: Liturgy Training Publications, 2012. (Also available on the Vatican website.)

Pope Benedict XVI. *The Word of the Lord* (*Verbum Domini*), Postsynodal Apostolic Exhortation. Boston: Pauline Books & Media, 2010.

National Conference of Catholic Bishops. "Criteria for the Evaluation of Inclusive Language Translations of Scriptural Texts Proposed for Liturgical Use." 1990. In *The Liturgy Documents, Volume Two: Second Edition; Essential Documents for Parish Sacramental Rites and Other Liturgies*. Chicago: Liturgy Training Publications, 2012.

Consilium for Implementing the Constitution on the Sacred Liturgy. *Comme le Prévoit*, On the Translation of Liturgical Texts for Celebrations with a Congregation. 1969. In *The Liturgy Documents, Volume Three,*

Foundational Documents on the Origins and Implementation of "Sacrosanctum Concilium." Chicago: Liturgy Training Publications, 2012.

Editions of the Lectionary

(The following are editions published by Liturgy Training Publications. Other publishers have also published the Lectionary in both ritual and study editions.)

Ritual Editions

National Conference of Catholic Bishops. *Lectionary for Mass for Use in the Dioceses of the United States of America.* 2nd typical ed.

Vol. 1, Sundays, Solemnities, Feasts of the Lord and the Saints,

Year A. Chicago: Liturgy Training Publications, 1998.

Year B. Chicago: Liturgy Training Publications, 1998.

Year C. Chicago: Liturgy Training Publications, 1998.

Vol. 2, Weekdays, Year 1, Proper of Saints, Common of Saints. Chicago: Liturgy Training Publications, 2001.

Vol. 3, Weekdays, Year 2, Proper of Saints, Common of Saints. Chicago: Liturgy Training Publications, 2001.

Vol. 4, Common of Saints, Ritual Masses, Masses for Various Needs, Votive Masses, Masses for the Dead. Chicago: Liturgy Training Publications, 2001.

Study Editions

Lectionary for Mass: Sundays, Solemnities, Feasts of the Lord and the Saints. Study ed. Chicago: Liturgy Training Publications, 1999.

Lectionary for Mass: Weekdays, Proper of Saints, Common of Saints, Ritual Masses, Masses for Various Needs, Votive masses, Masses for the Dead. Study ed. Chicago: Liturgy Training Publications, 2002.

Books and Articles

Boisclair, Regina. "The Lectionary: A Canon within the Canon." In *Anselm Academic Study Bible*, 77–83. Winona, MN: Anselm Academic, Christian Brothers Publications, 2013.

Bonneau, Normand. *The Sunday Lectionary: Ritual Word, Pascal Shape.* Collegeville, MN: Liturgical Press, 1998.

Bugnini, Annibale. *The Reform of the Liturgy 1948–1975.* Translated by Matthew J. O'Connell. Collegeville, MN: Liturgical Press, 1990.

Connell, Martin. *Hear the Word of the Lord: A Guide to the Lectionary.* Chicago: Liturgy Training Publications, 2015.

Just, Felix. The Catholic Lectionary Website. 1999–2012. http://catholic-resources.org/Lectionary/.

———. *The Lectionary: A Treasure for Liturgy and Prayer.* Audio CD. Now You Know Media, 2010.

Leclerc, Thomas L. "The Sunday Lectionary as Biblical Interpreter." *Liturgical Ministry* 13 (Fall, 2004): 169–80.

Schuller, Eileen. "Some Criteria for the Choice of Scripture Texts in the Roman Lectionary." In *Shaping English Liturgy*, edited by P. Finn and J. Schellman, 385–404. Washington, DC: Pastoral Press, 1990.

———. "Women in the Lectionary." *National Bulletin on Liturgy* 27, no. 137 (1994): 108–14.

Sloyan, Gerard. "Overview of the Lectionary for Mass: Introduction." In *The Bible Documents: A Parish Resource.* Chicago: Liturgy Training Publications, 2001.

———. *Preaching from the Lectionary: An Exegetical Commentary with CD-ROM.* Minneapolis: Fortress, 2004.

———. "What Kind of Canon Do the Lectionaries Constitute?" *Biblical Theology Bulletin: A Journal of Bible and Theology* 25, no. 1 (2000): 3–13.

West, Fritz. *Scripture and Memory: The Ecumenical Hermeneutic of the Three-Year Lectionary.* Collegeville, MN: Liturgical Press, 1997.

White, James. *Christian Worship in Transition.* Nashville: Abingdon, 1976.

NOTES

NOTES

NOTES

NOTES

NOTES

NOTES

NOTES